MW00388335

# THE MINISTRY OF HEALING

BY

A. J. (ADONIRAM JUDSON) GORDON

Chicago
FLEMING H. REVELL
1882

**CROSSREACH PUBLICATIONS**

*Hope. Inspiration. Trust.*

*WE'RE SOCIAL! FOLLOW US FOR NEW TITLES AND DEALS:*
FACEBOOK.COM/CROSSREACHPUBLICATIONS
@CROSSREACHPUB

**AVAILABLE IN PAPERBACK AND EBOOK EDITIONS**
PLEASE GO ONLINE FOR MORE GREAT TITLES
AVAILABLE THROUGH CROSSREACH PUBLICATIONS.
AND IF YOU ENJOYED THIS BOOK PLEASE CONSIDER LEAVING A
REVIEW ON AMAZON. THAT HELPS US OUT A LOT. THANKS.

© 2017 CROSSREACH PUBLICATIONS
ALL RIGHTS RESERVED, INCLUDING THE RIGHT TO REPRODUCE
THIS BOOK OR PORTIONS THEREOF IN ANY FORM WHATEVER.

# CONTENTS

# INTRODUCTION TO THE MODERN CROSSREACH EDITION

We are pleased here at CrossReach Publications to bring this important historical and scholarly work back into print for the modern reader.

For most of our works this is the first time they have been fully digitized and updated into a modern format in paperback *and* eBook editions for a general reading public to enjoy. Some have never been republished until now and some have only been published as poor photographic reproductions of the originals.

We are proud of the fact that our publications therefore are one of the most readable editions of these works on the market. All original spelling is usually retained unless stated otherwise, except for obvious spelling mistakes.

Most of our works also retain the original footnote numbering systems as they appeared in the original works, which will explain any unusual numbering you spot on the page. But don't worry, the footnotes are still logical and easy to follow.

We try our best within our limits to create faithful reproductions and are always happy to receive feedback or corrections on our editions. You will find our email and social media details at the end of the book.

The Team
CrossReach Publications

# Chapter 1

# THE QUESTION AND ITS BEARINGS, INTRODUCTORY

Have there been any miracles since the days of the Apostles? To this question the common answer has been, in our times at least, a decided no. A call recently put forth in one of our religious journals, asking the opinion of ministers, teachers, and theological professors on this point was very largely answered; and the respondents were well-nigh unanimous in the opinion that the age of miracles passed away with the apostolic period. The statement contained in several of these replies gave evidence indeed that the question had never been deeply investigated by the witnesses. In some instances there was a perhaps unintentional evading of the issue by the question "What is a miracle?" But there were only one or two replies which gave countenance to the view that miracles are possible in all ages, and have appeared more or less numerously in every period of the Church's history. If, then, the little book which we now send forth shall win any assent for its views, it will not do so, in all probability, because its sentiments accord with the opinion of the majority of the theologians of the day.

It is therefore no enviable task which we have undertaken. The demand of the times is rather in the contrary direction from that in which our conviction carries us. "The strongest requirement now pressing on the Church is for an adaptation of Christianity to the age,"—so we read not long since. How presumptuous it will look, in the face of such an utterance, for one to set his face squarely in the opposite direction, and insist that the greatest present demand is for the adaptation of the age to Christianity. And not that exactly; for "this present evil age" can never be made to harmonize with a religion that is entirely heavenly in its origin, in its course, and in its consummation. But we trust it will not be presumption to say that the Church in every direction needs to be reshaped to the apostolic model, and reinvested with her apostolic powers. For is it not apparent that between the indignant clamor of sceptics against primitive miracles, and the stern frowning of theologians upon any alleged modern miracles, the Lord's people are in danger of being frightened out of their faith in the supernatural? We speak of what we have often noticed. A simple-hearted believer comes into the assembly of the Church and details some remarkable answer to prayer—prayer for healing or prayer for deliverance—in response to which he alleges that God has wrought marvelously; and then we notice the slowness and shyness with which Christians turn their ears to the story, and the glances of embarrassment amounting almost to shamefacedness which they cast towards the minister, as though appealing for rescue from the perilous neighborhood of fanaticism to which they have been drawn. This we have often observed, and on it we have pondered, and from it we have raised the question again and again whether the Church has not drifted into an unseemly cautiousness concerning the miraculous. As a religion which is ritual is sure to put vestments on her ministers sooner or later, so a religion which is rational rather than spiritual will be certain to put vestments on the Lord's providences, insisting on their being draped in the habiliments of decent cause and effect, and attired in the surplice of natural law and order, lest God should "make bare His holy arm in the eyes of all the nations." "The world dislikes the recurrence of miracles." Yes, without question. For the world which "by wisdom knew not God" is very jealous of everything which it cannot explain or reproduce. "A miracle is something very embarrassing to mock professors." Doubtless; for it brings such people uncomfortably near to God. Accustomed only to such manifestations of the Infinite as have been softened and assuaged by passing through the medium of the natural, they cannot bear this close proximity to the Cause of causes. "He that is near to me is near to the fire" is one of the sayings which Apocrypha puts into the mouth of Christ. How shall they whose feet have never put off their shoes of rationalism and worldliness come near the burning bush, and into open vision of the "I AM"?

But it is not worldlings and false professors alone that dislike miracles. Real true-hearted and sincere disciples are afraid of them, and inclined to push away with quick impatience any mention of their possible occurrence in our time. In most cases probably this aversion comes from a wholesome fear of fanaticism.

On which point permit us to observe,—that fanaticism is in most instances simply the eccentric action of doctrines that have been loosened from their connection with the Christian system. Every truth needs the steadiness and equipoise which come from its being bound into harmony with all other truths. If the Church by her neglect or denial of any real doctrine of the faith thrusts that doctrine out into isolation and contempt, thus compelling it to become the property of some special sect, she need not be surprised if it loses its balance. She has deprived it of the conserving influence which comes from contact and communion with other and central doctrines, and so doomed it inevitably to irregular manifestations. If the whole body of Christians had been faithful to such truths as that of the second coming of Christ, and scriptural holiness, for example, we probably should never have heard of the fanaticism of Adventism and perfectionism. Let a fragment be thrown off from the most orderly planet, and it will whirl and rush through space till it is heated hot by its own momentum. It is nothing against a doctrine in our minds, therefore, that it has engendered fanaticism. One who studies the history of important religious revivals, indeed, must take quite an opposite view, and suspect that it is a proof of the vitality of the truth around which it has gathered.

Who that is acquainted with the religious movements led by Luther and Wesley, and with the endless extravagances that followed in their wake does not see that in the instances the stir produced came from the writhing of wounded error rather than from the birth of falsehood, from the contortions of the strangled serpents around the cradle of the new Hercules come for reformation. So let us be less disturbed by the unaccustomed stir of truth than by the propriety of dead and decent error.

But we are offering no apology for fanaticism and providing no place for it in connection with the doctrine we are defending. It need have no place. We believe in regeneration, the work in which God comes into immediate contact with the soul for its renewal. That is no less a miracle than healing in which God comes into immediate contact with the body for its recovery. In the one case there is a direct communication of the divine life to the Spirit, which Neander calls "the standing miracle of the ages"; in the other there is a direct communication of the divine health to the body which in the beginning was called "a miracle of healing." An able writer has said, we believe with exact truth: "You ask God to perform as real a miracle when you ask Him to cure your soul of sin as you do when you ask Him to cure your body of a fever."[1] Yet who of us thinks of encouraging fanaticism by preaching and praying for man's regeneration? Enthusiasm has often kindled about this truth, indeed, when it has had to be revived after long neglect and denial, but not when it has been held in orderly and recognized relation to other cardinal doctrines.

Very beautifully did one say of the sister of the poet Wordsworth, that "it was she who couched his eye to the beauties of nature." More than anything else is it needed today that some one couch the eyes of Christians to the realities of the supernatural. Holden of unbelief, filmed with suspicion and distrust, how many of the Lord's truest servants would be unable to discern His hand if He were to put it forth in miracles! It is not easy for those whose daily bread has always been forthcoming, with no occasion for the raven's ministration, to believe in miraculous feeding. The eyes that "stand out with fatness" would be the last ones to catch sight of the angels if they should chance to be sent with bread to some starving disciple. To whom says the Lord, "Anoint your eyes with eye-salve, that you may see"? Is it not to those that say, "I am rich and increased in goods, and in need of nothing"? If, then, we protest that we do not see what others claim to have witnessed of the Lord's outstretched hand, it may because of a Laodicean self-satisfaction into which we have fallen. When shall we learn that "the secret of the Lord is with them that fear Him" most deeply, and not of necessity with those who have studied the doctrines most deeply? And so, if the eyes long unused to any sight of the Lord's wonder-working are to be couched to the realities of the supernatural, it may be some very humble agent that shall perform the work,—some saintly Dorothea of Mannedorf at whose feet theologians sit to learn things which their utmost wisdom had failed to grasp, or some Catharine of Siena who speaks to learned ecclesiastics with such depth of insight that they exclaim with astonishment, "Never man spoke like this woman." In other words, let us not be too reluctant to admit that some of God's children in sore poverty

---

[1] Jellett: "Efficacy of Prayer"; Donnellan Lectures, 1877, P.43.

and trial and distress, and with the keener faith which such conditions have developed, may have had dealings with God of which we know nothing. At all events, be not angry, O you wise and prudent, at those Christians of simple faith who believe with strong confidence that they have had the Savior's healing touch laid upon them.

Nor should we unwittingly limit the Lord by our too confident theories about the cessation of miracles. The rationalist, jealous of any suggestion that God in these days may cross the boundary line that divides the natural from the supernatural, cries out against "the dogma of Divine interference," as he names it. The traditionalist, viewing with equal jealousy any notion that the Lord may pass the line that separates the apostolic from the non-apostolic age, and still act in His office of miracle working, sounds the cry of fanaticism. But what if some meantime should begin to talk about "the crown rights of Immanuel," as the old Covenanters did, insisting on His prerogative to work what He will, and when He will, and how He will, without our compelling it to be said of us and of our century that "He could not do many mighty works among them because of their unbelief"? Certainly the time has come for us to make use of all the Divine assistance that is within our reach. If there are any residuary legacies of power and privilege accruing to us since the fathers fell asleep, and yet remaining unclaimed, every consideration is pressing us to come forward and take possession of them. For observe what confessions of weakness our Protestant Churches are unconsciously putting forth on every hand. Note the dependence which is placed on artistic music, on expensive edifices, on culture and eloquence in the pulpit; on literary and social entertainments for drawing in the people, and on fairs and festivals for paying expenses. Hear the reports that come in at any annual convention of Churches, of the new organs and frescoings and furnishings, and of the—not saints' festivals—but strawberry festivals and ice cream festivals and flower festivals and the large results therefrom accruing. And all this from Churches that count themselves to be the body of Christ and the habitation of God through the Spirit! Is not this an infinite descent from the primitive records of power and success—the Lord "confirming the word with signs following," and the preaching which was "not with enticing words of man's wisdom, but in demonstration of the Spirit and of power"?

How deeply we need the demonstration of the Spirit in these days! We have not utterly lost it, indeed. When men are renewed by the Holy Ghost, and give the world the exhibition of a life utterly and instantly transformed, that is a master-stroke for our divine religion. "And that is all we want," most will say. But did such ever witness an instance of a drunkard cured in a moment of enslaving appetite by the prayer of faith—the opium habit which had baffled for years every device of the physicians broken and utterly eradicated by the direct energy of God's Spirit—the consumptive brought back from the edge of the grave, or the blind made to see by the same power, after long years of darkness—and the glowing love, the exultant thankfulness, the fervid consecration which almost invariably follow such gracious deliverances? If they have not, they have not witnessed a sight that has within our own time and knowledge extorted conviction from the most reluctant witnesses.

These are some of the practical bearings of the question before us.

It is not our purpose in this volume to define a miracle any further than we have already done so. For the definitions generally given are widely variant; and it is easy for a disputant to evade facts by entrenching himself behind a definition. We prefer rather to appeal to specimens of acknowledged miracles, and then to press the question whether there have been any like them in modern days. It is written in the Acts of the Apostles as follows: "And it came to pass, that the father of Publius lay sick of a fever and of a bloody flux; to whom Paul entered in and prayed and laid his hands on him, and healed him."[2] This is conceded, we suppose, to be a miracle of healing. Has anything of the same sort occurred in the Church since the days of the apostles?

Again it is written in the same book: "And a certain man lame from his mother's womb was carried, whom they laid daily at the gate of the temple which is called Beautiful, to ask alms of them that entered into the temple: who, seeing Peter and John about to go into the temple, asked an alms. And Peter, fastening his eyes upon him with John, said, Look on us. And he gave heed unto them, expecting to receive something of them. Then Peter said, silver and gold have I none; but such as I have give I thee: In the name of Jesus Christ of Nazareth, rise up and walk. And he took him by the right hand, and lifted him up: and immediately his feet and ankle bones received strength. And he leaping up stood, and walked, and entered with them into the temple, walking, and leaping, and praising God." Acts 3:2, 8.

This transaction is expressly called a "miracle of healing" in the same Scripture. Has there been any recurrence of such a miracle since the time of Christ's immediate disciples? It has been our purpose in preparing the present volume to let the history of the Church of all ages answer to the teaching of Scripture on this question without presuming to dogmatize upon it ourselves.

One who has not committed himself on this subject, as it was the fortune of the writer to do a year ago in a little tract called "The Ministry of Healing," has several things to learn. First, that there is a sensitiveness amounting often to extreme irritability towards any who venture to disturb the traditional view of this question. Credulity is sure to get more censure than honest doubt; and while one may with impunity fall behind the accepted standard of faith concerning the supernatural, provided he does it in a regretfully necessitous spirit, it is hardly safe for one to go beyond that standard. Thus a little experience has made us aware of the peril to which we have exposed ourselves of being sorely shot at by the theological archers. But being defamed we still entreat our critics to deal

---

[2] Acts 28: 8.

kindly and candidly with us, since we desire nothing but the furtherance of the truth.

But in another way one has a real advantage who has published his views on such a question. His communication puts him en rapport with those like minded, and opens to him sources of information which he could not otherwise have had. It has been an occasion of no little surprise to us to learn how widely the minds of Christians of all names and countries are exercised upon this subject. Information to this effect has come to us not only in the constant testimonies from humble Christians who bear witness to what God has wrought in their own bodies; but also from pastors and evangelists and Bible readers and foreign missionaries, and in one instance from a theological professor, expressing their strong assent to the view which is herein set forth. We are well aware, indeed, that it is not a question of human opinion, but of Scriptural testimony. In the Word of God, therefore, we wish our argument to lean its heaviest weight. The witnesses whom we have brought forward from the Church of all the ages have been summoned only that they may corroborate this Word.

May the Lord graciously use whatever of truth there may be in this volume for the comfort and blessing of His children; may He mercifully pardon whatever of error or forwardness of opinion it may contain. And if by His blessing and furtherance our words should bring a ray of hope to any who are sick, let not those who are "whole" and who "need not a physician " unreasonably grudge their suffering and afflicted brethren this boon of comfort.

# Chapter 2
# THE TESTIMONY OF SCRIPTURE

In the atonement of Christ there seems to be a foundation laid for faith in bodily healing. Seems, we say, for the passage to which we refer is so profound and unsearchable in its meaning that one would be very careful not to speak dogmatically in regard to it. But it is at least a deep and suggestive truth that we have Christ set before us as the Sickness-bearer as well as the Sin-bearer of His people. In the gospel it is written, "And He cast out devils and healed all that were sick, that it might be fulfilled which was spoken by Esaias the prophet, saying, Himself took our infirmities and bare our sicknesses." Matt. 8: 17. Something more than sympathetic fellowship with our sufferings is evidently referred to here. The yoke of His cross, by which He lifted our iniquities, took hold also of our diseases; so that it is in some sense true that as God "made Him to be sin for us who knew no sin," so He made Him to be sick for us who knew no sickness. He who entered into mysterious sympathy with our pain, which is the fruit of sin, also put Himself underneath our pain, which is the penalty of sin. In other words, the passage seems to teach that Christ endured vicariously our diseases as well as our iniquities.[3]

If, now, it be true that our Redeemer and Substitute bore our sicknesses, it would be natural to reason at once that He bore them that we might not bear them. And this inference is especially strengthened from the fact that when the Lord Jesus removed the burden of disease from "all that were sick," we are told that it was done "that the scripture might be fulfilled, Himself took our infirmities and bare our sicknesses." Let us remember what our theology is in regard to atonement for sin. "Christ bore your sins, that you might be delivered from them," we say to the penitent. Not sympathy—a suffering with, but substitution—a suffering for, is our doctrine of the Cross; and therefore we urge the transgressor to accept the Lord Jesus as his Sin-bearer, that he may himself

---

[3] Dr. Hovey commenting on this passage says: "The words quoted by the evangelist are descriptive in the original passage of vicarious suffering. It is next to impossible to understand them otherwise. Hence in the miraculous healing of disease, a fruit if not a penalty of sin, Jesus appears to have had a full sense of the evil and pain which He removed. His anguish in the garden and on the cross was but the culmination of that which He felt almost daily while healing the sick, cleansing the leprous, or forgiving the penitent. By the holy sharpness of His vision He pierced quite through the veil of sense and natural cause, and saw the moral evil, the black root of all disorder, the source of all bodily suffering. He could therefore heal neither bodily nor spiritual disease without a deep consciousness of His special relation to man as the Substitute, the Redeemer, the Lamb of God who was to bear the penalty of the world's guilt."—"The Miracles of Christ," p. 120.

no longer have to bear the pains and penalties of his disobedience. But should we shrink utterly from reasoning thus concerning Christ as our Pain-bearer? We do so argue to some extent at least. For we hold that in its ultimate consequences the atonement affects the body as well as the soul of man. Sanctification is the consummation of Christ's redemptive work for the soul; and resurrection is the consummation of His redemptive work for the body. And these meet and are fulfilled at the coming and kingdom of Christ.

But there is a vast intermediate work of cleansing and renewal effected for the soul. Is there none of healing and recovery for the body? Here, to make it plain, is the Cross of Christ; yonder is the Corning of Christ. These are the two piers of redemption spanned by the entire dispensation of the Spirit and by all the ordinances and offices of the gospel. At the cross we read this twofold declaration

"Who His own self bare our sins."

"Himself bare our sicknesses."

At the coming we find this twofold work promised:

"The sanctification of the Spirit."

"The redemption of the body."

The work of sanctification for the spirit stretches on from the cross to the crown, progressive and increasing until it is completed. Does the work of the body's redemption touch only at these two remote points? Has the gospel no office of healing and blessing to proclaim meantime for the physical part of man's nature? In answering this question we only make the following suggestions, which point significantly in one direction.

Christ's ministry was a twofold ministry, affecting constantly the souls and the bodies of men. "Thy sins are forgiven thee," and "Be whole of thy plague," are parallel announcements of the Savior's work which are found constantly running on side by side.

The ministry of the apostles, under the guidance of the Comforter, is the exact facsimile of the Master's. Preaching the kingdom and healing the sick, redemption for the soul and deliverance for the body,—these are its great offices and announcements. Certain great promises of the gospel have this double reference to pardon and cure. The commission for the world's evangelization bids its messengers stretch out their hands to the sinner with the message, "He that believeth shall be saved," and to "lay hands on the sick and they shall recover." The promise by James, concerning the prayer of faith, is that it "shall save the sick, and if he have committed sins they shall be forgiven him." Thus this twofold ministry of remission of sins and remission of sickness extends through the days of Christ and that of the apostles.

We only suggest these facts, leaving the example and acts and promises of the Lord and His apostles to stretch out their silent index in the direction which our argument will obediently pursue throughout this discussion.

Only one other fact need be alluded to—the subtle, mysterious, and clearly recognized relation of sin and disease. The ghastly flag of leprosy, flung out in the face of Miriam, told instantly that the pirate sin had captured her heart. Not less truly did the crimson glow of health announce her forgiveness when afterwards the Lord had pardoned her and restored her to his fellowship. And it is obvious at once that our Redeemer cannot forgive and eradicate sin without in the same act disentangling the roots which that sin has struck into our mortal bodies.

He is the second Adam come to repair the ruin of the first. And in order to accomplish this He will follow the lines of man's transgression back to their origin, and forward to their remotest issue. He will pursue the serpent trail of sin, dispensing His forgiveness and compassion as He goes, until at last He finds the wages of sin and dies its death on the cross; and He will follow the wretched track of disease with His healing and recovery, until in His resurrection He shall exhibit to the world the firstfruits of these redeemed bodies, in which "this corruptible shall have put on incorruption and this mortal shall have put on immortality."

From this mysterious and solemn doctrine of the gospel, let us turn now to some of its clear and explicit promises.

We will take first the words of the gospel according to Mark: "These signs shall follow them that believe: in my name shall they cast out devils; they shall speak with other tongues; they shall take up serpents; and if they drink any deadly thing it shall not hurt them; they shall lay their hands on the sick and they shall recover." Mark 16:17, 18.

It is important to observe that this rich cluster of miraculous promises all hangs by a single stem—faith. And this is not some exclusive or esoteric faith. The same believing to which is attached the promise of salvation has joined to it also the promise of miraculous working. Nor is there any ground for limiting this promise to apostolic times and apostolic men, as has been so violently attempted. The links of the covenant are very securely forged,—"He that believeth and is baptized shall be saved," in any and every age of the Christian dispensation. So with one consent the Church has interpreted the words, "And these signs shall follow them that believe," in every generation and period of the Church's history;—so the language compels us to conclude.

And let us not unbraid this twofold cord of promise, holding fast to the first strand because we know how to use it, and flinging the other back to the apostles because we know not how to use it. When our Lord gives command to the twelve, as He sends them forth, "to heal all manner of sickness and all manner of diseases," we might conclude that this was an apostolic commission, and one which we could not be warranted in applying to ourselves. But here the promise is not only to the apostles, but to those who should believe on Christ through the word of these apostles; or, as Bullinger the Reformer very neatly puts it in his comment on the passage, to "both the Lord's disciples and the disciples of the

Lord's disciples."[4] Whatever practical difficulties we may have in regard to the fulfilment of this word, these ought not to lead us to limit it where the Lord has not limited it. For if reason or tradition throws one half of this illustrious promise into eclipse, the danger is that the other half may become involved. Indeed, we shall not soon forget the cogency with which we heard a skillful sceptic use this text against one who held the common opinion concerning it. Urged to "believe on the Lord Jesus Christ," that he might be saved, he answered: "How can I be sure that this part of the promise will be kept with me, when, as you admit, the other part is not kept with the Church of today?" And certainly, standing on the traditional ground, one must be dumb before such reasoning. The only safe position is to assert emphatically the perpetuity of the promise, and with the same emphasis to admit the general weakness and failure of the Church's faith, in appropriating it.[5] For who does not see that a confession of human inability is a far safer and more rational refuge for the Christian than an implication of the divine changeableness and limitation? There is a phrase of the Apostle Paul which has always struck us as containing marvelous keenness and wisdom, if not covert irony—"What the law could not do in that it was weak through the flesh." The law must not be impugned by even a suspicion: "the law of the Lord is perfect." But there has been utter failure under its working—the perfection which it requires has not appeared. Rashly and dangerously, it would seem, the apostle has arraigned the law, telling us what it "could not do" and wherein it was "weak "—and then, having brought us to the perilous edge of disloyalty, he suddenly turns and puts the whole fault on us where it belongs—"What the law could not do in that it was weak through the flesh." The one weak spot in the law is human nature; there is where the break is sure to come; there is where the fault is sure to lie. In like manner this great promise, with which Christ's commission is enriched and authenticated, has failed only through our unbelief. It is weak through the weakness of our faith, and inoperative through lack of our cooperating obedience.[6] We believe, therefore, that whatever difficulties there may be in us, there is but one attitude for us to take as expounders of the Scripture—that of unqualified assent.

---

[4] "Et discipuli Domini, et discipulorum Domini discipuli." And to show his belief in the fulfilment of the promise, Bullinger adds, "To this the Acts of the Apostles bear witness. Ecclesiastical history bears witness to the same. Lastly, the present times bear witness; wherein through confidence in the name of Christ numbers greatly afflicted and shattered with disease are restored afresh to health."

[5] "The reason why many miracles are not now wrought is not so much because faith is established, as that unbelief reigns."—Bengel.

[6] It is the want of faith in our age which is the greatest hindrance to the stronger and more marked appearance of that miraculous power which is working here and there in quiet concealment. " Unbelief is the final and most important reason for the retrogression of miracles."—Christlieb, "Modern Doubt," p. 336.

The treatment which the Commentator Stier gives to this passage is truly refreshing. It is a brawny Saxon exegesis laying hold of a text, to cling to it, not to cull from it; to crown it with an amen! not to condition it with a date. For he puts the two sayings side by side and bids us look at them: "He that believeth shall be saved;". . . "Them that believe . . . . these signs shall follow." And then he gives us these strong words: "Both the one and the other apply to ourselves down to the present day, and indeed for all future time. Everyone applies the first part of the saying to ourselves—teaching everywhere that faith and baptism are necessary in all ages to salvation, and that unbelief in all ages excludes from it. But what right has any to separate the words that Jesus immediately added from His former words? Where is it said that these former words have reference to all men and all Christians, but that the promised signs which should follow those who believe referred solely to the Christians of the first age? What God hath joined together, let no man put asunder."

It should be observed, however, that while the same word is employed in both clauses of this text, there is a change in number from the singular to the plural form. "He that believeth and is baptized shall be saved." The promise of eternal life is to personal faith, and to every individual on the ground of his faith. "Them that believe, these signs shall follow." The promise of miracles is to the faithful as a body. The Church has come into existence so soon as any have believed and been baptized; and thus this guarantee of miraculous signs seems to be to the Church in its corporate capacity. "Are all workers of miracles? have all the gifts of healing? do all speak with tongues?" asks the apostle. No, but some employ these offices, so that the gifts are found in the Church as a whole. For the Church is "the body of Christ," and to vindicate its oneness with the Head it will do the things which He did, as well as speak the words which He spoke. How significant the place where this promise is found! It was given just as the Lord was to be received up into heaven to become "Head over all things to His Church." It is Elijah's mantle let fall upon Elisha; so that having this, the disciple can repeat the miracles of the Master. O timid Church, praying for a "double portion of the Spirit," 2 Kings 2:9, 15, of the ascending Prophet, and having His promise, "Greater works than these shall ye do, because I go to my Father," and yet afraid to claim even a fragment of His miracle-working power! We conclude, therefore, that this text teaches that the miraculous gifts were bestowed to abide in the Church to the end, though not that every believer should be endowed with them.

This promise given in Mark emerges in performance in the Acts of the Apostles. But it is significant and to be carefully observed that the miraculous gifts are not found exclusively in the hands of the Apostles. Stephen and Philip and Barnabas exercised them. These did not belong to the Twelve—to that special and separated body of disciples with whom it has been said that the gifts were intended to remain. It was not Stephen an apostle, but "Stephen a man full of faith and of the Holy Ghost"—"Stephen full of faith and power," that "did great wonders and miracles among the people." Acts 6:5, 8. We in these days cannot be apostles; but we are commanded to be "filled with the Spirit," and therefore are at least required and enjoined to have Stephen's qualifications. According to the teaching in Corinthians, it is as members of Christ's body and partakers of His Spirit that we receive these truths.[7]

We come now to consider the promise in James 5:14, 15. "Is any sick among you? Let him call for the elders of the Church; and let them pray over him, anointing him with oil in the name of the Lord. And the prayer of faith shall save the sick, and the Lord shall raise him up: and if he have committed sins they shall be forgiven him."

Now let us note the presumption there is that this passage refers to an established and perpetual usage in the Church.

That command in the great commission—"Baptizing them in the name of the Father, and of the Son, and of the Holy Ghost," appears in the Acts of the Apostles in constant exercise; and in the letters of the apostles as explained, unfolded, and enforced. Rom. 6:3, 4; Col. 2:12; 1 Peter 3:21.

The injunction given at the institution of the Supper—"This do in remembrance of me," appears in the Acts of the Apostles in constant exercise; and in the letters of the apostles as explained and unfolded and enforced. Acts 2:46; 1 Cor. 10:11.

The promise given also in the great commission—"They shall lay their hands on the sick and they shall recover," appears in the Acts of the Apostles in constant exercise; and in the letters of the apostles as explained, unfolded, and enforced. 1 Cor. 12:29; James 5:14, 15. Thus this office, like the great ordinances of Christianity, rests on the threefold support of promise and practice and precept. And we cannot too strongly emphasize this fact—that what was given by our Lord in promise before His ascension should appear as an established usage in the Church after His ascension. For we all insist that the Church of the apostles was the model for all time. When we are called "followers of the Lord," we might rightly protest that, though His followers, we surely could not be expected to walk in His steps as He enters the field of the miraculous. When we hear Paul saying, "Be ye followers of me, as I am of Christ," we might well insist that we could not imitate him in working wonders, since he is an apostle and we only humble disciples. But when we read, "For ye brethren became followers of the Churches of God which in Judea are in Christ," we say, "Yes!" in every point and punctilio; for these are the pattern for all churches in all time. So we all hold and

---

[7] "You say that Christ Jesus and His Apostles and Messengers were endued with power from on high not only to preach the word for conversion but also with power of casting out devils and healing bodily diseases. I answer, as a holy witness of Christ Jesus once answered a Bishop—"I am a member of Christ Jesus as well as Peter himself." The least Believer and Follower of Jesus partakes of the nature and spirit of Him their holy Head and Husband, as well as the strongest and holiest that ever did or suffered for His holy name."—Roger Williams, "Experiments of Spiritual Life and Health," 1652.

teach. We believe that there is nothing in all the ordering and furniture of the church which was present in the beginning which should be absent now. And if we rejoice in having the laver and the bread of the ordinances, the ministry of the word and prayer, not the less should we, willingly be without the primitive miraculous gifts which were like the Shekinah glory, the outward visible signs of God's presence among His people.

# Chapter 3
# THE TESTIMONY OF REASON

"Nowise contrary to Scripture, and very agreeable to reason," is the opinion with which Archbishop Tillotson closes his observations on the recurrence of Christian miracles in modern times.

It may be asked what reason has to do with such a question: nothing except as corroborating the testimony of faith. Miracles have not been generally defended on the ground of their intrinsic reasonableness, but on that of their scriptural authority; and that in us which first assents to their reality is not so much the logical mind as the docile heart—"the heart proffering itself by humiliation to inspiration," as Pascal expresses it. And yet we hold that to believe in miracles is reasonable, after it is faithful. That supreme miracle, the resurrection of our Lord, was first credited and published by loving and devoted believers; but it has since been defended again and again by Christian philosophers. So, then, reason is not forbidden to look into the empty tomb and see the folded graveclothes and therefrom to conclude that Christ is risen, only she must be accompanied by faith, and not be surprised if faith like that "other disciple" shall outrun her and come first to the sepulcher. John 20:4.

Believing miracles to have existed in the days of Christ and the apostles, is it reasonable to conclude that they may have continued to exist until our own time? It seems to us that it is.

For in the first place, if they should cease they would form quite a distinct exception to everything else which the Lord introduced by His ministry. The doctrines which He promulgated and which His apostles preached—atonement, justification, sanctification, and redemption—have never been abrogated or modified. The ordinances which He enjoined—Baptism and the Lord's Supper—have never been repealed. The Divine operations in the soul, which He ordained for man's recovery from the fall—"the washing of regeneration and the renewing of the Holy Ghost "—have never been suspended. These belong to the dispensation of grace which Jesus Christ introduced, and which is to span the whole period between His first and His second advents. All orthodox Christians hold them to be perpetual and unchangeable.

And not only so; there was to be a development of these doctrines and operations of Christianity under the administration of the Spirit, so that the stream which started with Christ's ministry was to widen and deepen under the ministry of those who should come after Him. "I have many things to say unto you, but ye cannot bear them now; howbeit when He the Spirit of Truth is come, He will guide you into all truth"—an enlargement of knowledge and a development of doctrine under the ministry of the Comforter rather than a decrease!

"Verily, verily, I say unto you, He that believeth on me, the works that I do shall he do also, and greater works than these shall he do, because I go unto my Father," John 14:12,—a reinforcement of power for service rather than an abatement! And all intelligent Christians admit that these promises were fulfilled in the wider unfolding of truth and the more extensive work of regeneration which have occurred under the administration of the Spirit.

The law of Christianity is from less to greater, and not from greater to less. "Of all that Jesus began both to do and teach until the day in which He was taken up" are the significant words with which the Acts of the Apostles opens; and as the beginnings are less than the unfoldings, we may conclude that the Lord was to do more through the Spirit's ministry than through His own. And so far as works of regeneration and salvation are concerned this undoubtedly proved true, and is proving just as true today. The conversion of three thousand souls in a single day under Peter's preaching surpasses anything which occurred in the earthly ministry of Christ; and the conversion of ten thousand in a year on a single mission field in India also surpasses the results of any single year in the Savior's ministry.

Now, as the "works" of Christ are among the things which He "began to do," miracles of healing stood side by side with miracles of regeneration, and therefore we say that the theory of the "gradual cessation" of miracles contradicts all analogy. We have read of certain South African rivers which, instead of beginning as tiny brooks and flowing on deepening and widening as they go, burst out from prolific springs and then become shallower and shallower as they flow on until they are lost in the wastes of sand without ever reaching the sea. Two streams of blessings started from the personal ministry of our Lord—a stream of healing and a stream of regeneration; the one for the recovery of the body and the other for the recovery of the soul—and these two flowed on side by side through the apostolic age. Is it quite reasonable to suppose that the purpose of God was that one should run on through the whole dispensation of the Spirit and that the other should fade away and utterly disappear within a single generation? We cannot think so.

If miracles were abnormal manifestations of Divine power, against nature as well as above nature, they might indeed be expected to cease; for the abnormal is not as a rule perpetual. The earthquakes and volcanoes, nature's agues and fever fits, are soon over; but the sunshine and the rain, the breezes and the blossoms, nature's tokens of health, are perennial. And miracles of healing are manifestations of nature's perfect health and wholeness, lucid intervals granted to our deranged and suffering humanity. They are not catastrophes, but exhibitions of that Divine order which shall be brought in when our redemption is completed. We cannot for a moment admit the complaint of sceptics that miracles are an infraction of the laws of nature. Alas for them! that they have so lost their ear for harmony that they cannot distinguish earth's wail from heaven's hallelujah; and know not the difference between the groans of a suffering creation and the music of the spheres, as it was on that day when "the morning stars sung together and all the sons of God shouted for joy"! Miracles of healing and dispossession are reminiscences of an unfallen Paradise and prophecies of a Paradise regained. Though we call them supernatural, they are not contranatural. "For surely," as one has said, "it is plainly contrary to nature and indeed most unnatural that one should have eyes and not see, ears and not hear, organs of speech and not speak, and limbs without the power to use them; but not that a Savior should come and loose his fetters. It was contrary to nature that ruthless death should sever the bands of love which God Himself has knit between mother and son, between brother and sister, but not that a young man of Nain or a Lazarus should be released from the fetters of death through a mighty word! And that was the climax of the unnatural that the world should nail the only righteous One to the cross; but not that the holy Bearer of that cross should conquer undeserved death, should rise and victoriously enter into His glory.[8]

If, then, miracles of healing are exhibitions of Divine recovery and order in nature, and not rude irruptions of disorder, why having been once begun should they entirely cease? We are under the dispensation of the Spirit, which we hold to be an unchangeable dispensation so long as it shall continue. On the day of Pentecost the Holy Spirit was installed in office to abide in the Church perpetually. Exactly as the first disciples were under the personal ministry of Christ, we are under the personal ministry of the Comforter. Having begun His miracles at Cana of Galilee, Jesus never permanently suspended them. His last gracious act before He was delivered into the hands of wicked men was to stretch forth His hand and heal the ear of the high priest's servant. And having wrought the first notable miracle after Pentecost by the hand of Peter at "the Beautiful gate," why should the Holy Ghost in a little while cease from His miraculous works? We know that the Lord "did not many mighty works" in a certain place "because of their unbelief," and that the place where He was thus hindered was "in His own country and in His own house." But we know not that He would not do mighty works in any place if faith were present; and were it not a simpler solution of this whole question to say that possibly Christ through the Holy Ghost will not do many miracles today on account of man's unbelief, than to say that He wills not to do them?

Then again the use which was made of miracles of healing as signs seems to argue strongly for their permanency. If the substance remains unchanged, why should the sign which was originally chosen to exhibit it be superseded?

It is said, indeed, with some show of reasonableness, that Christianity being a spiritual system, physical miracles were but the staging employed for the erection of that system, destined to fall away and disappear so soon as it should be

---

[8] Christlieb.

completed. That certainly might be so. But how do we regard the argument of those who have reasoned precisely thus about the ordinances of Christianity? The Friends and other bodies of religionists have said that the rites of Baptism and the Lord's Supper are too physical to be perpetuated in connection with a spiritual religion; that whatever place they may have had in the founding of Christianity, they are not demanded for its continuance. To which we reply at once—first, that they constitute a vivid sign and picture-writing of the great foundation facts of Christianity, the death and resurrection of our Lord; that they are a pledge and earnest of those great things to come at the resurrection of the just and the marriage supper of the Lamb, and that by the constant and glowing appeal which they make to the senses they tend to keep these facts in perpetual remembrance; and secondly, that however we may reason about it, these are ordinances, established for continual observance by the Lord until He come, and therefore we are forbidden to terminate them. This reasoning would be accepted, doubtless, as sound by all orthodox believers. But we can argue in precisely the same way about the "signs" which attested the first preaching of the Gospel. In the great commission we have them solemnly established as the accompaniments of preaching and believing the Gospel. In James's epistle we find healing recognized as an ordinance, just as in Paul's epistles to the Romans and to the Corinthians we find Baptism and the Supper recognized as ordinances. As signs they could never lose their significance until the Lord comes again; they pointed upward and told the world that Christ who had been crucified was alive and on the throne; they pointed forward and declared that He would come again and subdue all things unto Himself. This last we believe to be the chief testimony of miracles as signs: they were given to be witnesses to the "restitution of all things," which Christ shall accomplish at His coming and kingdom. For notice how invariably our Lord joins the commandment to heal the sick and to cast out devils with the commission to preach the kingdom, thus: "Jesus went about preaching the Gospel of the kingdom and healing all manner of sickness and all manner of disease amongst the people." "And as ye go preach, saying, The Kingdom of Heaven is at hand. Heal the sick; cleanse the lepers; raise the dead; cast out devils." Matt. 4:23; Matt. 10:7; read also Luke 9:1 and 10:9. Healing and resurrection and the casting out of demons were a kind of firstfruits of the kingdom, to be presented along with its announcement. As, to use a familiar illustration, the commercial traveler carries samples of his goods as he goes forth soliciting trade, the Lord would have His ministers carry specimens and tokens of the kingdom in their hands as they go forth to preach that kingdom.[9]

---

[9] "The devil is said to be he who has the power of death: he is the author of death; he introduced sin into the world, and through sin death; and as he is the author of death, so he is the author of disease, which is just a form of death, and which, as well as death, is the work of the devil. And, therefore, Jesus while He was upon the earth healed the

This seems to be what is referred to in that picture of the groaning creation which we find in the eighth chapter of Romans: "But ourselves, also, which have the firstfruits of the Spirit, even we ourselves groan within ourselves, waiting for the adoption, to wit the redemption of the body." Rom. 8:23. As though it were said: We have witnessed the works of the Spirit in healing the body of its sicknesses, in dispossessing it of the evil spirit, in quickening it from the power of death; and this makes us long only the more for that crowning and consummated work of the Spirit of which these things are but an earnest, when "he that raised up Jesus from the dead shall quicken your mortal bodies by His Spirit that dwelleth in you." These signs were the fore-tokens of the body's redemption which the Lord at the first bade His messengers carry with them as they went forth preaching Jesus and the resurrection. Even dumb, suffering nature would be made glad by the sight of them. Goethe beautifully says, "Often have I had the sensation as if nature in wailing sadness entreated something of me, so that not to understand what she longed for cut me to the heart." But we understand what she longs for, "For we know that the whole creation groaneth and travaileth in pain together until now, waiting for the adoption, to wit the redemption of the body." And they who "have tasted the powers of the world to come" were bidden to go forth and preach the kingdom, bearing in their hands the grapes of Eshcol, which they have brought from that kingdom, that they may show what a goodly land that is where "the inhabitants shall no more say, I am sick." Thus, not only our wounded and pain-stricken humanity shall be cheered with the hope of better things, but even dumb nature shall be comforted by these foregleams of that millennium wherein "the creature itself also shall be delivered from the bondage of corruption into the glorious liberty of the children of God."[10]

Now, why, if these credentials were so rigidly attached to the first preaching of the kingdom, should they utterly disappear from its later proclamation? There is the same groaning of creation to be answered; the same coming of the King to be announced; the same unrepealed commission of the Master to be carried out. The answer given by the majority to this question is, "Signs are no longer

---

sick and raised the dead, not merely to typify a spiritual healing and quickening, but to prove that He was indeed the promised Deliverer by destroying the works of the devil, and also to give a foretaste and a shadow of the ultimate effect of His redemption upon the whole man, body and soul. And thus we find in the New Testament that the healing of the sick and the preaching of the Gospel of the kingdom are almost always conjoined, and are so spoken of as though they meant the same thing." Thos. Erskine, "Brazen Serpent," p. 272.

[10] "Sickness is sin apparent in the body, the presentiment of death, the forerunner of corruption. Disease of every kind is mortality begun. Now, as Christ came to destroy death, and will yet redeem the body from the bondage of corruption, if the Church is to have a firstfruits or earnest of this power it must be by receiving power over diseases which are the firstfruits and earnest of death." Edward Irving, "Works," v., 464.

needed." If reason can be satisfied with this answer, faith cannot. For "faith has its reasons, which reason cannot understand." Among these is this: "Jesus Christ, the same yesterday, today, and forever." Miracles we hold to be a shadow of good things to come. The good thing to come for the soul is its full and perfect sanctification at the appearing of the Lord. The work of regeneration and daily renewal by the Holy Ghost is the constant reminder and pledge and preparation for that event; and regeneration is a "perpetual miracle." The good thing to come for the body is "glorified corporeity," resurrection and transformation into Christ's perfect likeness when He shall appear. Healing by the power of the Holy Ghost is the pledge and foretoken of this consummation. Was it in God's purpose that we should never again witness this after the apostolic age was past?

Here let us answer three or four objections which have been urged against our position. "If you insist that miracles of healing are possible in this age, then," it is said, " you must logically admit that such miracles as raising the dead, turning water into wine, and speaking in unknown tongues, are still possible." But it requires only a casual glance to see that healing through the prayer of faith stands on an entirely different basis from any of these other miracles.

Raising the dead is nowhere promised as a privilege or possibility for the believers of today. There is indeed in one instance (Matt. 10:8) a command to raise the dead; but this was given specifically to the twelve, and in a temporary commission. It therefore differs very materially from the promise in Mark 16, which was to all believers, and is contained in a commission which was for the entire dispensation of the Spirit. That the Lord did this miracle, and that His apostles did it, in one or two instances is not enough. Unless we can show some specific promise given to the Church as a whole, we are bound to concede that such works are not for us or for our age. Healing the sick, on the contrary, rests on a distinct and specific promise to believers.

Miracles on external nature, like the turning of water into wine, and the multiplying of the loaves, belong exclusively to the Lord; we do not find them perpetuated beyond His own ministry either in fact or in promise. Miracles of cure, on the contrary being in the direct line of the Lord's redemptive work, abound in he ministry of the disciples as they do in that of the Lord, and have the clear pledge of Scripture for their performance. The discrimination which Godet makes between miracles of healing and those performed on the outward world we believe to be strictly accurate. He says: "One consequence of the close connection of soul and body is that when the spirit of man is in this way vivified by the power of God it can sometimes exert upon the body, and through it upon other bodies, an influence which is marvelous. This kind of miracle is therefore possible in every age of the Church's history; it was possible in the middle ages, and is possible still. That which would seem to be no longer possible is the miraculous action of the Divine power upon external nature. The age of such miracles seems to have closed with the work of revelation, of which they were but the auxiliaries." "Defense of the Christian Faith," p. 208.

As to miracles of prophecy, we see no reason to believe that they were strictly limited to apostolic times. We recall, indeed, the one important text on this question, "But whether there be prophecies, they shall fail; whether there be tongues, they shall cease; whether there be knowledge, it shall vanish away; for we know in part, and we prophesy in part, but when that which is perfect is come, then that which is in part shall be done away." Thus speaks the Spirit in the Epistle to the Corinthians.

By this scripture some have attempted to shut up all miracles within the apostolic era, as belonging to the things which were "in part," and therefore destined to pass away. But, in the first place, let it be noted that it is only prophecies, tongues, and knowledge that are specified, not healings; and we are to put no more within this limitation than the Word of God has put there. And, in the second place, the bounds set to the exercise of these gifts is "when that which is perfect is come," which scholarship has generally held to mean when the Lord Himself shall return to earth.[11]

The gifts of tongues and of prophecy therefore do not seem to be confined within the first age of the Church. We cannot forget, indeed, that the utterances of prophecy and knowledge culminated and found their highest expression when the canon of the New Testament Scriptures was completed; so that some thoughtful expositors have conjectured that this may have been the coming of that which is perfect so far as prophecy and knowledge are concerned. But in either event this does not touch the gifts of healing. These cannot have culminated so long as sickness and demoniacal possession are unchecked in the world, nor until the great Healer and Restorer shall return from above.

To sum up these observations then: is it reasonable to conclude that the office of healing through faith, resting on the same apostolic example, and held by the same tenure of Divine promise and precept as the other functions of the Christian ministry, was alone destined to pass away and disappear within a single generation? With the advance in power and knowledge which was to take place under the administration of the Holy Spirit after Pentecost, is it reasonable to believe that in this one particular instance there was designed to be a signal retarding of supernatural energy? Is the Lord less likely to heal those who extend to Him the touch of faith now that He is on the right hand of God, having all power in heaven and earth given to Him, than He was while on earth?

> "Is the truce broke? or cause we have
> A Mediator now with Thee,
> Dost Thou therefore old treatyes wave,
> And by appeales from Him decree?
> Or is 't so, as some green heads say,

---

[11] 1 Cor. 13:10. "This verse shows by the emphatic "then" that the time when the gifts shall cease is the end of this dispensation. The imperfect shall not cease till the perfect is brought in." Ellicott.

# A. J. Gordon

That now all miracles must cease?
Though Thou hast promised they should stay
The tokens of the Church, and peace."
Henry Vaughan, 1654.

Is it reasonable to believe that the administration of the Comforter has changed since its first inauguration, so that, while His mission and His offices were to continue until the end of this age, it is found that one of His ministries has entirely disappeared since the days of the apostles? With sin and sickness still holding sway in the world, is it reasonable to consider the latter as entirely beyond the redemptive work of Christ, while the former is so entirely met by that work, which was not the case in the beginning? And, finally, until the harvest shall come, is it reasonable to suppose that we are to be left entirely without the firstfruits of our redemption? Until we can answer these questions, perhaps caution is becoming us, at least, in denying that miracles of healing are still wrought.

# Chapter 4
# THE TESTIMONY OF THE CHURCH

Witnesses who are above suspicion leave no room for doubt that the miraculous powers of the apostolic age continued to operate at least into the third century." Such is the conclusion of Dr. Gerhard Uhlhorn; and one who has read the work from which this opinion is taken will not doubt his eminent fitness to judge of such a question. "Conflict of Christianity with Heathenism," p. 169. This concession is a very important one in its bearings on this whole subject. Prove that miracles were wrought, for example, in the second century after Christ, and no reason can be thereafter urged why they might not be wrought in the nineteenth century. The apostolic age, it must be admitted, was a peculiarly favored one. So long as the men were still living who had seen the Lord, and had companied with Him during His earthly ministry, there were possible secrets of power in their possession that a later generation might not have. It is easy to see, therefore, that this period might be especially distinguished by the gifts of the Spirit.

And yet the Savior seems to be careful to teach that there would be an augmenting rather than a diminishing of supernatural energy after His departure. "But ye shall receive power after that the Holy Ghost is come upon you." "Verily, verily I say unto you, he that believeth on me the works that I do shall he do also, and greater works than these shall he do: because I go to my Father." Acts 1:9; John 14:12. He made no provision for the arrest of the stream of Divine manifestations which He had started, either in the next age or in a subsequent age. But, conceding certain marked advantages possessed by the immediate followers of Christ, if we find in history that there is no abrupt termination of miracles with the expiration of the apostolic age, then we must begin to raise the question why there should be any termination at all, so long as the Church remains and the ministry of the Spirit is perpetuated?

Now, when we turn to the writings of the Christian Fathers, as they are called, we find the testimonies abundant to the continuance of the miraculous powers. We will quote only a few as specimens from a large number, which may be readily collated by any one who will take the pains. Justin Martyr says: "For numberless demoniacs throughout the whole world and in your city, many of our Christian men, exorcizing them in the name of Jesus Christ, who was crucified under Pontius Pilate, have healed, and do heal, rendering helpless and driving the possessing devils out of the men, though they could not be cured by all the other exorcists and those who used incantations and drugs." Apol. II.,. chap. vi.

Irenaeus says: ◆Wherefore also those who are in truth the disciples, receiving grace from Him, do in His name perform miracles so as to promote the welfare of others, according to the gift which each has received from Him."

Then after enumerating the various gifts he continues: "Others still heal the sick by laying their hands upon them, and they are made whole." Adv. Haer., Book II., iv.

Tertullian says: "For the clerk of one of them who was liable to be thrown upon the ground by an evil spirit was set free from his affliction, as was also the relative of another, and the little boy of a third. And how many men of rank, to say nothing of the common people, have been delivered from devils and healed of disease." Ad. Scap., IV., 4.

Origen says: "And some give evidence of their having received through their faith a marvelous power by the cures which they perform, invoking no other name over those who need their help than that of the God of all things and of Jesus, along with a mention of His history. For by these means we too have seen many persons freed from grievous calamities and from distractions of mind and madness, and countless other ills which could be cured neither by men nor devils." Contra Celsum, B. iii. chap. xxiv.

Clement says, in giving directions for visiting the sick and afflicted: "Let them, therefore, with fasting and prayer, make their intercessions, and not with the well arranged and fitly ordered words of learning, but as men who have received the gift of healing confidently to the glory of God." Epis. C. xii.

The weight of these and like testimonies is so generally acknowledged by Church historians that it seems little less than hardihood for scholars to go on repeating that well-worn phrase, "The age of miracles ended with the apostles." Mosheim, speaking of the fourth century, says: "But I cannot on the other hand assent to the opinion of those who maintain that in this century miracles had entirely ceased." Cent. iv.

Dr. Waterland says: "The miraculous gifts continued through the third century, at least."[12]

Dodwell declares that "though they generally ceased with the third century, there are several strongly attested cases in the fourth."

Dr. Marshall, the translator of Cyprian, says "there are successive evidences of them down to the age of Constantine."

"The age of Constantine" is a significant date at which to fix the termination of miracles. For almost all Church historians hold that there was a period when the simpler and purer forms of supernatural manifestation ceased to be generally recognized, or were supplanted by the gross and spurious types which characterize the Church of the middle ages.[13] And the era of Constantine's

---

[12] See list of citations in "Creation and Redemption" (London, 1877), p. 50.

[13] "With regard to the continuance of miracles after the apostolic age, we have testimonies, not only from Tertullian and Origen, who tell us that many in their time

conversion confessedly marks a decided transition from a purer to a more degenerate and worldly Christianity. From this period on, we find the Church ceasing to depend wholly on the Lord in heaven, and resting in the patronage and support of earthly rulers; ceasing to look ever for the coming and kingdom of Christ as the consummation of her hopes, and exulting in her present triumph and worldly splendor. Many of her preachers made bold to declare that the kingdom had come, and that the prophetic word "He shall have dominion from sea to sea, and from the river to the ends of the earth" had been fulfilled." * Eusebius, L. X., 3, 4.

If now, as we have indicated elsewhere, the miracles were signs of the sole kingship of the living and exalted Christ, and pledges of His coming again to subdue all things to Himself, it is not strange that as the substance of these truths faded from men's minds their sign should have gradually disappeared also. At all events it is very significant that precisely the same period, the first three centuries, is that generally named by historians as the era in which that apostolic hope "the glorious appearing of the great God and our Savior, Jesus Christ," and that apostolic faith, "they shall lay hands on the sick and they shall recover," remained in general exercise. It is not altogether strange, therefore, that when the Church forgot that "her citizenship is in heaven," and began to establish herself in luxury and splendor on earth, she should cease to exhibit the supernatural gifts of heaven. And there is a grim irony in the fact, that after death and the grave had gradually become the goal of the Christian's hope, instead of the personal coming of Christ, then we should begin to find miracles of healing alleged by means of contact with the bones of dead saints and martyrs, instead of miracles of healing through the prayer of faith offered to the living Christ. Such is the change introduced by the age of Constantine!

"Ah, Constantine; of how much ill was cause,
Not thy conversion, but those rich domains
That the first wealthy Pope received of thee." Dante.

But now comes a most suggestive fact: that wherever we find a revival of primitive faith and apostolic simplicity there we find a profession of the chaste and evangelical miracles which characterized the apostolic age. These attend the cradle of every spiritual reformation, as they did the birth of the Church herself. Waldenses, Moravians, Huguenots, Covenanters, Friends, Baptists, and Methodists all have their record of them.

Hear the following frank and simple confession of the Waldenses, that people who for so many ages kept the virgin's lamp trimmed and burning amid the gross darkness with which the harlot had overspread the people: "Therefore,

---

were convinced, against their will, of the truths of Christianity by miraculous visions, but also, much later, from Theodore of Mopsueste (429). The latter says: 'Many heathen amongst us are being healed by Christians from whatever sickness they have, so abundant are miracles in our midst.'" Christlieb, "Modern Doubt," p. 321.

concerning this anointing of the sick, we hold it as an article of faith, and profess sincerely from the heart, that sick persons, when they ask it, may lawfully be anointed with the anointing oil by one who joins with them in praying that it may be efficacious to the healing of the body according to the design and end and effect mentioned by the apostles; and we profess that such an anointing performed according to the apostolic design and practice will be healing and profitable. Johannis Lukawitz, "Waldensis Confessio," 1431. See also "Waldensia," p. 25.

Then after condemning extreme unction, that sacrament of the Papists wherein an ordinance for life is perverted into an ordinance for death, they say further: "Albeit we confess that the anointing of the sick performed according to the design, end, and purpose of the apostles, and according to their practice and power, of which St. Mark and James make mention, is lawful; and if any priest possessing the grace of healings have so anointed the sick and they have recovered, we would exhort all that when they are really ill they omit not to receive that ordinance at their hands, and in no way despise it, because despisers of that or of other ordinances, so far as they are ordained by Christ, are to be punished and corrected, according to the rules of the evangelical law."

The Moravians, or United Brethren, as they are otherwise called, have obtained a good report among all Christians for their simple piety, and especially for their fervent missionary zeal. They have not only been earnest reformers, but reformers of reformers; so that such men as Wesley, catching their light and getting kindled by it, have brought a new revival to the backslidden children of the Reformation. On principles already referred to, we might expect to find their missionary zeal signalized by supernatural tokens. And so it has been, if we may believe what seem to be trustworthy records. In what is regarded as a very faithful history of the United Brethren—that of Rev. A. Bost—the author gives his own view of the continuance of the apostolic gifts in a very clear manner, and records for us with equal clearness the sentiments of the Moravians. He says:

"We are, indeed, well aware that, so far from its being possible to prove by Scripture, or by experience, that visions and dreams, the gift of miracles, healings, and other extraordinary gifts, have absolutely ceased in Christendom since the apostolic times, it is on the contrary proved, both by facts and by Scripture, that there may always be these gifts where there is faith, and that they will never be entirely detached from it. We need only take care to discern the true from the false, and to distinguish from miracles proceeding from the Holy Ghost, lying miracles, or those which without being so decidedly of the devil do not so decidedly indicate the presence of the Lord." Bost, i., p. 17.

In this book are several statements of the Brethren concerning the character and discipline of their churches. The famous Zinzendorf writes as follows: "To believe against hope is the root of the gift of miracles; and I owe this testimony to our beloved Church, that apostolic powers are there manifested. We have had undeniable proofs thereof in the unequivocal discovery of things, persons, and circumstances, which could not humanly have been discovered, in the healing of maladies in themselves incurable, such as cancers, consumptions, when the patient was in the agonies of death, etc., all by means of prayer, or of a single word." Bost, i., p. III.

Speaking of the year 1730, he says:

"At this juncture various supernatural gifts were manifested in the Church, and miraculous cures were wrought. The brethren and sisters believed what the Savior had said respecting the efficacy of prayer, and when any object strongly interested them they used to speak to Him about it, and to trust in Him as capable of all good; then it was done unto them according to their faith. The count (Zinzendorf) rejoiced at it with all his heart, and silently praised the Savior who thus willingly condescended to what is poor and little. In this freedom of the brethren towards our Savior Jesus Christ, he recognized a fruit of the Spirit, concerning which they ought on no account to make themselves uneasy, whoever it might be, but rather to respect Him. At the same time he did not wish the brethren and sisters to make too much noise about these matters, and regard them as extraordinary; but when, for example, a brother was cured of disease, even of the worst kind, by a single word or by some prayer, he viewed this as a very simple matter, calling to mind ever that saying of Scripture, that signs were not for those who believed, but for those who believed not." Idem, pp. 405-6.

Thus we have the sentiment of the Moravians on the subject of Miracles very distinctly indicated. And the statements quite accord with their simple faith and filial confidence in the Lord, as indicated in other things.

The following furnishes a very beautiful glimpse into the actual miraculous experiences above referred to:

"Jean de Platteville had a childlike confidence in our Savior's promise to hear His children's prayers. Of this he often had experience. One example we will here offer:—A married sister became extremely ill at Herrnhut. The physician had given up all hopes, and her husband was plunged in grief. Watteville visited the patient, found her joyfully expecting her removal, and took his leave, after having encouraged her in this happy frame. It was at that time still the custom of unmarried brethren, on Sunday evening, to go about singing hymns before the brethren's houses, with an instrumental accompaniment. Watteville made them sing some appropriate hymns under the window of the sick sister, at the same time praying in his heart to the Lord that He would be pleased, if He thought good, to restore her to health. He conceived a hope of this so full of sweetness and faith that he sang with confidence these lines:

"Sacred Cross, O sacred Cross!
Where my Savior died for me,
From my soul, redeemed from loss,
Bursts a flame of love to Thee.

When I reach my dying hour

Only let them speak Thy name;
By its all-prevailing power
Back my voice returns again.'

"What was the astonishment of those who surrounded the bed of this dying sister when they saw her sit up, and join with a tone of animation in singing the last line—

"Back my voice returns again."

"To his great amazement and delight he found her, on ascending to her chamber, quite well. She recovered perfectly, and not till thirty-five years after did he attend her earthly tabernacle to its final resting-place."

And now we come to the testimony of that most illustrious band of Christian worthies, the Scotch Covenanters. Illustrious, we said, and yet with a light altogether ancient, apostolic, and strange to our modern age. Let one read that book of thrilling religious adventure and heroic faith, "The Scots Worthies," and he will almost seem to be perusing the Acts of the Apostles reacted. Such sterling fortitude—such mighty prayers—such conquests of preaching and intercession! Howie, its author, seems to have had in mind especially, in writing it, the rebuke it would bring to a later faithless and degenerate age, by showing, as he says in his preface, "how at the peril of their lives they brought Christ into our hands," and "how quickly their offspring are gone out of the way piping and dancing after a golden calf." Nor did he think such a luxurious and unbelieving generation would be able to credit these mighty deeds of their fathers. For he continues: "Some may be ready to object that many things related in this collection smell too much of enthusiasm; and that other things are beyond all credit. But these we must suppose to be either quite ignorant of what the Lord did for our forefathers in former times, or else, in a great measure, destitute of the like gracious influences of the Spirit by which they were actuated and sustained." If we are inclined to discredit the marvels of Divine interposition recorded in this book, we have to remember that the men who relate them, and of whom they are related, are the historic characters of the Scottish Kirk—Knox, Wishart, Livingston, Welch, Baillie, Peden, and Craig. We never tire of repeating the great and holy things which these men did in other fields of spiritual service. Who has not heard how John Livingston preached with such extraordinary demonstration of the Spirit that five hundred souls were quickened or converted under a single sermon? And what Christian has not had his spiritual indolence rebuked by reading of John Welch rising many times in the night to plead for his flock, and spending seven and eight hours a day in Gethsemane intercessions for the Church and for lost souls? These things we have read and repeated without incredulity. But how few have read or dared to repeat the story of the same John Welch praying over the body of a young man, who, after a long wasting sickness, "has closed his eyes and expired to the apprehension of all spectators,"—how, in spite of the remonstrance of friends, he held on for three hours, twelve hours, twenty-five, thirty-six, forty-eight hours, and when at last it was insisted that the "cold dead" body should be borne out to burial how he begged for an hour more,—and how, at the end of that time, he "called upon his friends and showed them the dead young man restored to life again, to their great astonishment"? All this is told with the utmost detail in the book of Scots Worthies. If we are startled to ask in amazement—as who will not be?—"Are such things possible in modern times?" we might better begin with the question, Has such praying and resistless importunity with God ever been heard of in modern times? If we can get a miraculous faith the miraculous works will be easy enough to credit. Yet this is a specimen of the men who compose this extraordinary group of Christian heroes.

The wonders recorded of them are of every kind—marvels of courage; marvels of faith, marvels of martyrdom, and marvels of prophetic foresight. Theirs was a faith born and nourished of the bitterest persecution. But if, according to the saying of their biographer, they were "followed by the prophet's shadow, the hatred of wicked men," it is equally true that they were crowned with the apostle's halo, the power of the Holy Spirit.

Here we read of the holy Robert Bruce, of whom the beautiful incident is told, that once being late in appearing in his pulpit a messenger was sent for him, who reported—"I think he will not come today, for I overheard him say to another, 'I protest I will not go unless Thou goest with me.' Howbeit, in a little time he came, accompanied by no man, butfull of the blessing of Christ; for his speech was with much evidence and demonstration of the Spirit." Of this man, mighty in pulpit prayers, it is affirmed that "persons distracted, and those who were past recovery with falling sickness, were brought to him and were, after prayer by him on their behalf, fully restored from their malady." P. 118. Also we read of Patrick Simpson, whose insane wife, from raving and blaspheming as with demoniacal possession, was so wonderfully healed by his importunate prayers that the event was found thus gratefully recorded upon some of the books of his library: "Remember, O my soul, and never forget the 16th of August, 1601, what consolation the Lord gave thee, and how He performed what He spoke according to Zechariah, 'Is not this a brand plucked out of the fire?'" P.116.

We give verbatim one incident of healing as recorded in this book, admonishing the reader that this story, as well as several others, has been somewhat softened in later editions of the work, with the avowed purpose of making it accord more exactly with modern religious sentiments. It is from the life of John Scrimgeour, minister of Kinghorn in Fife, and "an eminent wrestler with God":

"Mr. Scrimgeour had several friends and children taken away by death: and his only daughter who at that time survived, and whom he dearly loved, being seized with the King's evil, by which she was reduced to the point of death, so that he was called up to see her die; and finding her in this condition he went out into the fields (as he himself told) in the nighttime in great grief and anxiety, and began to expostulate with the Lord, with such expressions as, for all the world, he durst not again utter. In a fit of displeasure he said—'Thou, O Lord, knowest that I have been serving Thee in the uprightness of my heart according to my power and measure: nor have I stood in awe to declare Thy mind even unto the greatest in the time; and Thou seest that I take pleasure in this child. Oh that I could obtain such a thing at Thy hand as to spare her!' and being in great agony of spirit at last it was said to him from the Lord—'I have heard thee at this time, but use not the like boldness in time coming for such particulars.' When he came home the child was recovered, and sitting up in the bed took some meat: and when he looked on her arm it was perfectly whole." Edinburgh Ed., 1812, pp. 89, 90.

Now, when we reflect that these things are recorded by the pen of some of the holiest men the Church of God has ever seen; and recorded, too, as the experience of their own ministry of faith and prayer, the fact must at least furnish food for reflection to those who continue to assert with such confident assurance that the age of miracles is past. Past it may be indeed, if the age of faith is past. For that we conceive to be the real question. It is not geography or chronology that determines the boundary lines of the supernatural. It is not apostolic men that make an apostolic age, not a certain date of Anno Domini. We are for ever thinking to turn back the shadow certain degrees upon the dial, to bring again the age of miracles, forgetting that He who is "without variableness or the shadow of turning" has said, "If you can believe"—not if you were born in Palestine and within the early limits of the first Christian century—"all things are possible to him that believes." When by the stress of violent persecution or by the sore discipline of reproach and rejection by the world the old faith is revived, then we catch glimpses once more of the apostolic age. And such, perhaps, beyond all others in modern times, was the age of the Covenanters.

No one can read this stirring narrative of their sufferings and triumphs, their martyrdoms and miracles, without a profound spiritual quickening. There is little danger withal of the book ministering to fanaticism, for if any one should be inspired by it with an ambition to be a miracle-worker he will meet the challenge on every page—"Are you able to drink the cup that I drink of, and to be baptized with the baptism that I am baptized with?"

If we come to the Huguenots, those faithful followers of the Lamb, among generations that were so greedily and wantonly following the Dragon, we get glimpses of the same wonderful things. In the story of their suffering and obedience to the faith in the mountains of Cevennes, whither they had fled from their pursuers upon the revocation of the edict of Nantes, we hear constant mention of the exercise of miraculous gifts. There were Divine healings and extraordinary actings of the Spirit in quickening and inspiration. They who in their exile carried their mechanical arts and inventions into England to the great blessing of the nation, carried here and there the lost arts of supernatural healing, to the wonder of the Church of Christ. "Morning Watch," B. iv., p. 383.

Among the early Friends, as is well known, the same manifestations were constantly reported. Whatever we may think of the general teaching of this sect, no one can read the Journal of George Fox without feeling that he was a devoted man of God, doing a wholesome work of quickening and rebuke in a time of great spiritual deadness and conformity to the world. His quaint prayer that he "might be baptized into a sense of all conditions" seems to have been literally fulfilled. Like a latter day apostle he went among all ranks, rebuking the gay and worldly, turning away the wrath of those at enmity, visiting the sick and ministering to the prisoner. A worthy model is he for any minister, in any age, who would learn how to labor "in season, out of season" for the Lord.

Not only in his teaching but especially in his active service does he recognize the continuous operation of the Spirit in miraculous ministries. He records these manifestations without comment, as though they were as much a matter of course as conversion or regeneration.

In a record of evangelizing in Twy-Cross in Lincolnshire, England, he says: "Now there was in that town a great man that had long lain sick and was given over by the physicians: and some friends in that town desired me to go and see him, and I went up to him in his chamber and spoke the word of life to him, and was moved to pray for him, and the Lord was entreated and restored him to health." Journal, B. i., p. III.

While preaching in Hertfordshire, they told him of a sick woman and requested him to go to her help. He says: "John Rush of Bedfordshire went along with me to visit her, and when we came in, there were many people in the house that were tender about her: and they told me she was not a woman for this world, but if I had anything to comfort her concerning the world to come I might speak to her. So I was moved of the Lord to speak to her, and the Lord raised her up again, to the astonishment of the town and country." Id., vol. I., p. 281.

This book abounds in such instances, told without ostentation or enlargement, but almost always alluded to as "Miracles."

In the earlier days of the Baptists, days of simplicity and purity, we meet with similar illustrations of miraculous faith and manifestation. As usual, it was in times of great straits, when the prison doors were shut upon the persecuted flock, that the windows of heaven were opened in miraculous blessing.

Vavasor Powell, "the morning star of the Welsh Baptists," as he has been named, has left a clear affidavit to his faith and practice on the subject we are considering. He was a man of the same fiber as the Covenanters; endued with such power of the Spirit that extraordinary revivals followed his preaching wherever he went. He was also a bitter sufferer for the faith—having in the course of his life lain in thirteen different prisons for his testimony for Christ.

Besides the uncommon blessing which attended his preaching it is recorded that "many persons were recovered from dangerous sickness through the prayer of faith which he offered." He took the promise in James 5 literally, as shown in the story of his own recovery, and especially as declared in the following article of his creed—"Visiting the sick and for the elders to anoint them in the name of the Lord is a gospel ordinance and not repealed." Ivimy's "History of the Baptists," p. 333. That his creed was to some extent adopted by the English Baptists appears from the account given in the same book of the ceremony of anointing and prayer as performed for a blind woman at Aldgate in London. Rev. Hansard Knollys, and Rev. Henry Jessey, eminent names in the early ministry of the body, united with others in the service, prayer being offered and the words pronounced, "The Lord Jesus restore thee thy sight." Idem, p. 332.

Among the Methodists we find references here and there to the appearance of miraculous manifestations in the churches. There is one very striking instance which is recorded of Ann Mather, daughter of Joseph Benson the Methodist commentator, the story being given in full by the father in his journal. She had been afflicted with lameness in the feet, for some years having no use of her limbs, and not for a long time having walked a step. We give the narrative in the words of Mr. Benson's Journal, abridging in unimportant details:

"Oct.4th. This evening the Lord has shown us an extraordinary instance of His love and power. My dear Ann yet remained without any use of either her limbs, and indeed without the least feeling of them, or ability to walk a step, or lay the least weight upon them, nor had she any use of them for upward of twelve months. I was very much afraid that the sinews would be contracted, and that she would lose the use of them forever. We prayed, however, incessantly, that this might not be the case; but that it would please the Lord, for the sake of her three little children, to restore her.

"This day a part of my family and some of my pious friends went to take tea at her house; Mr. Mather bringing her down in his arms into the dining-room. After tea I spoke of the certainty of God's hearing the prayer of His faithful people, and repeated many of his promises to that purpose. I also enlarged on Christ's being the same yesterday, today, and forever, and still both able and willing to give relief to His afflicted people: that though He had doubtless done many of His miracles of healing chiefly to prove Himself to be the Messiah, yet that He did not do them for that end only, but also to grant relief to human misery, out of His great compassion for suffering mankind; and that not a few of His other miracles of mercy He had wrought principally or only for this latter purpose, and that He was still full of compassion for the miserable. I then said, 'Ann, before we go to prayer, we will sing the hymn which was full of consolation to your mother,' and I gave out the words of the hymn beginning

"Thy arm, Lord, is not shortened now,
It wants not now the power to save;
Still present with Thy people, Thou," etc.

"After singing, we then kneeled down to pray, and Ann took her infant child to give it the breast, that it might not disturb us with crying while we were engaged in prayer, I prayed first, and then Mr. McDonald, all the company joining fervently in our supplications. We pleaded in prayer the Lord's promises, and especially that He has said that whatever two or three of His people should agree to ask, it should be done for them (Matt. 17:19). Immediately on our rising from our knees, Ann beckoned to the nurse to take the child, and then instantly rose up, and said, 'I can walk, I feel I can'; and proceeded half over the room: when her husband, afraid she should fall, stepped to her, saying, 'My dear Ann, what are you about?'

"She put him off with her hands, saying, 'I don't need you: I can walk alone,' and then walked three times over the floor; after which, going to a corner, she knelt down and said, 'Oh let us give God thanks!' We kneeled down, and gave thanks; Ann continuing on her knees all the time, at least twenty minutes; she then came to me, and with a flood of tears threw her arms about my neck, and then did the same first to one of her sisters, then to the other, and afterwards to Mrs. Dickenson; every one in the room shedding tears of gratitude and joy. She then desired her husband's brother to come upstairs; and when he entered the room she cried out, 'Adam, I can walk;' and to show him that she could, immediately walked over the floor and back again.

"It was indeed the most affecting scene I ever witnessed in my life. She afterward, without any help, walked upstairs into her lodging-room, and with her husband kneeling down, joined in prayer and praise.

"In conversation with her afterward, I learned from her the following particulars;—that when she was brought into the diningroom a little stool was put under her feet, but which she felt no more than if her feet had been dead. While we were singing the hymn, she conceived faith that the Lord would heal her; began to feel the stool, and pushed it away; then set her feet on the floor, and felt that; while we prayed she felt a persuasion she could walk, and felt inclined to rise up with the child in her arms; but thinking to do that would be thought rash, she delayed till we had done praying, and then immediately rose up, and walked as above related."

Among the persons present who witnessed this remarkable scene was Rev. James McDonald, who followed Mr. Benson in prayer, and was afterwards his biographer; and in making reference to this wonderful healing he says: "All believed that the power to walk, which she received in an instant, was communicated by an immediate act of omnipotence." The account was also published in the Methodist Magazine, from which this is quoted.

We have thus set before us a mass of evidence for the continuance of miraculous interventions which few, we imagine, would wish to condemn as utterly false. Whatever deduction or allowance any may wish to make, there remains too solid a substratum of well-proven fact to be easily set aside. Untimely—born out of due season—is the objection which will at once be urged, indeed. That is to say, put the same facts and the same witnesses back into the age of the apostles and they can be easily enough credited, but not as speaking for modern times. But some believe that the Church, like the tree of life "whose leaves are for the healing of the nations," not only bears twelve manner of fruits but "yields her fruit every month." "All supernatural manifestations determined with apostolic times and apostolic men"—so I read from a learned author, as I glanced for a moment from the page which I was writing. Then casting another glance through my window I saw a tree just before me crowned with a fresh coat of green leaves and white blossoms. Strange sight to witness in the month of October! Yet such was the season in which it came to pass. For it had happened that the canker worms had stripped the tree of all its foliage and left it bare and naked; but because there was life in its veins and the sap had not yet returned downward, it must find expression, and so even in autumn it had leaved and blossomed.

Alas that the Church should ever have been shorn of her primitive beauty! But so it was: apostasy succeeding to purity, and papacy to apostasy, and corruption to papacy, and infidelity to corruption, till it was literally as the prophet has written: "That which the palmer-worm hath left, hath the locust eaten; and that which the locust hath left, hath the canker-worm eaten, and that which the canker-worm hath left, hath the caterpillar eaten." Joel 1:4.

But because there is life still remaining in the Church, because the sap has not utterly departed from the tree of God, fresh shoots are constantly putting out bearing the leaves and blossoms of primitive piety, and not less certainly the rich fruits of miraculous blessing. And so we are persuaded it shall be until the end. For it belongs to the Church as the body of Christ to do the works of Christ, and it belongs to believers as the habitation of the Spirit to manifest the gifts and fruits of the Spirit.

# Chapter 5
# THE TESTIMONY OF THEOLOGIANS

Admitting, with the historians, that miracles ceased to be recognized in the Church, as a whole, after the third century, there have still continued to be witnesses here and there to their occurrence through all the ages. We call to the stand several theologians, who have not only defended the doctrine of the continuance of miracles, but have cited illustrations of what they regarded as credible instances in support of their theory.

Augustine, it has been claimed, denied the existence of miraculous interpositions in his day; and he certainly said some things that give occasion for that opinion. But, on the other hand, he has left on record what cannot but be regarded as the strongest testimony to their continuance in his generation. Archbishop Trench considers that the true solution of this seeming contradiction is, that he held to their cessation in his earlier writings, and, changing his opinion, maintained their continuance in his later.[14]

If this be so, we must take the last opinion as his true conviction, not that which he had retracted. How decidedly, indeed, he commits himself to the doctrine of the perpetuity of miracles will appear if we read the heading of one of the chapters of the De Civitate Dei: "Concerning the miracles which were wrought in order that the world might believe in Christ, and which cease not to be wrought now that the world does believe." He lived in a time, indeed, when the shadows of superstition had already begun to creep over the Church, and the records of miracles which he makes are occasionally marred by some trace of such superstition:

"For even now," he says, "Miracles are wrought in His name, whether by the sacraments, or by prayers, or at the tombs of the saints. But they are not proclaimed with the same renown, so as to be spread abroad with the former. For the sacred volume which was to be made known on all sides caused the former to be told everywhere and to hold their place in all men's memories; but the latter are known of scarcely beyond the whole city or neighborhood where they may happen to be wrought." "Works," v., p. 299.

In the same chapter he goes on to give instances to corroborate this assertion. We reproduce one—abridging the narrative, which is very extended, but

---

[14] "In an early work, De Vera Religione, xxv. 47, he denies their continuance, while in his Retractions he withdraws this statement, or limits it to such miracles as those that accompanied baptism at the first. In De Civ. Dei., xxii. 8, he enumerates at great length miracles, chiefly those of healing, which he believed to have been wrought in his own time, and coming more or less within his own knowledge."—Trench, "Notes on the Miracles," P.59.

retaining the essential points. The story is exceedingly natural and affecting. It is concerning Innocentius, a devout Christian, and a man of high rank in Carthage. He was suffering from a painful malady, and had submitted to several surgical operations for its removal, but without effect. An eminent surgeon, Alexandrinus by name, being summoned, declared that there was no hope except possibly in another operation. This was decided on, and several officers of the Church were with him the evening before his trial, of whom he begged that they would be present the next day at what he feared would be his death. "Among those present," says Augustine, "was Aurelius, now the only survivor and a bishop: a man ever to be mentioned with the greatest regard and honor, with whom, in calling to mind the wonderful works of God, I have often conversed on the occurrence; and I find that he retains the fullest recollection of what I now relate." The rest we give in the words of Augustine:

"We then went to prayer; and, while we were kneeling and prostrating ourselves, as on other occasions, he also prostrated himself, as if someone had forcibly thrust him down, and began to pray: in what manner, with what earnestness, with what emotion, with what a flood of tears, with what agitation of his whole body, I might almost say with what suspension of his respiration, by his groans and sobs who shall attempt to describe? Whether the rest of the party were so little affected as to be able to pray I knew not. For my part I could not. This, alone, inwardly and briefly, I said: 'Lord, what prayers of Your own children will You ever grant if You grant not these?' For nothing seemed more possible but that he should die praying. We arose, and, after the benediction by the bishop, left him, but not until he had besought them to be with him in the morning, nor until they had exhorted him to calmness. The dreaded day arrived, and the servants of God attended as they had promised. The medical men make their appearance; all things required for such an occasion are got ready, and, amidst the terror and suspense of all present, the dreadful instruments are brought out. In the meantime, while those of the bystanders whose authority was the greatest endeavored to support the courage of the patient by words of comfort, he is placed in a convenient position for the operation, the dressings are opened, the seat of the disease is exposed, the surgeon inspects it, and tries to find the part to be operated upon with his instrument in his hand. He first looks for it, then examines by the touch; in a word, he makes every possible trial, and finds the place perfectly healed. The gladness, the praise, the thanksgiving to a compassionate and all-powerful God, which, with mingled joy and tears, now burst from the lips of all present, cannot be told by me. The scene may more easily be imagined than described."

It will be seen, on careful reading, that aside from the testimony of the writer himself, there is everything in this story to indicate the genuineness and authenticity of the miracle. Its detailed narration shows how unquestionably the writer believes in healing through the prayer of faith.

Martin Luther, "whose prose is a half battle," would be likely to speak strongly on this subject if he spoke at all. Martin Luther, whose prayers were victorious battles, so that they who knew him were wont to speak of him as "the man who can have whatever he wishes of God," would be likely to plead efficaciously in this field if he entered it at all. And so he did. The testimony of Luther's prayers for the healing of the body are among the strongest of any on record in modern times. He has been quoted, indeed, as disparaging miracles. And the explanation of this fact is perfectly easy for those who have investigated his real opinions. Like the other Reformers—like Huss and Latimer, for example—he revolted violently from the impudent miracles which in his day put forth their claims on every side. This frequently led him to speak in very contemptuous terms of modern signs and wonder-working. And it is not strange that some, lighting on these utterances, should have concluded that he denied all supernatural interventions in modern times. But if we turn from Luther the controversialist to Luther the pastor, we find a man who believed and spoke with all the vehemence of his Saxon heart on the side of present miracles. "How often has it happened and still does," he says, "that devils have been driven out in the name of Christ, also by calling on His name and prayer that the sick have been healed?" And he suited his action to his words on this point; for when they brought him a girl saying that she was possessed with a devil, Luther laid his hand on her head, appealed to the Lord's promise, "He that believeth on me the works I do shall he do also, and greater works than these shall he do," and then prayed to God, with the rest of the ministers of the Church, that, for Christ's sake, he would cast the devil out of this girl. Seckendorf's " History of Lutheranism," B. iii., p. 133. Perfect recovery is recorded in this instance, as well as in several others where he prayed for the sick.

The most notable instance is that of Philip Melancthon. An account of this recovery, which seems to be trustworthy, is given by the historian to whom we have just referred. Melancthon had fallen ill on a journey, and a messenger had been despatched to Luther. The story continues: "Luther arrived and found Philip about to give up the ghost. His eyes were set; his consciousness was almost gone; his speech had failed, and also his hearing; his face had fallen; he knew no one, and had ceased to take either solids or liquids. At this spectacle Luther was filled with the utmost consternation, and turning to his fellow-travelers said: 'Blessed Lord, how has the devil spoiled me of this instrument!' Then turning away towards the window he called most devoutly on God."

Then follows the substance of Luther's prayer: "He besought God to forbear, saying that he had struck work in order to urge upon Him in supplication, with all the promises he could repeat from Scripture; that He must hear and answer now if He would ever have the petitioner trust in Him again."

The narrative goes on: "After this, taking the hand of Philip, and well knowing what was the anxiety of his heart and conscience, he said, 'Be of good courage, Philip, thou shalt not die. Though God wanted not good reason to slay thee, yet

He willeth not the death of a sinner, but that he may be converted and live. Wherefore give not place to the spirit of grief, nor become the slayer of thyself, but trust in the Lord who is able to kill and to make alive.' While he uttered these things Philip began, as it were, to revive and to breathe, and gradually recovering his strength, was at last restored to health."

If the reader should conclude hastily that this recovery may be accounted for on entirely natural principles, we have to remind him that the conviction of both parties to the transaction was quite otherwise.

Melancthon writing to a friend says: "I should have been a dead man had I not been recalled from death itself by the coming of Luther."

Luther speaks in the same manner writing to friends: "Philip is very well after such an illness, for it was greater than I had supposed. I found him dead, but, by an evident miracle of God, he lives."

Again referring to his attendance at the Diet, he says: "Toil and labor have been lost, and money spent to no purpose; nevertheless, though I have succeeded in nothing, yet I fetched back Philip out of Hades, and intend to bring him now, rescued from the grave, home again with joy," etc.

Such is the witness of the great Reformer, and, if needful, it might be strengthened by reference to other remarkable instances of his power in prayer for the sick.

That of Myconius is well known, who wrote of himself: "Raised up in the year 1541 by the mandates, prayers, and letter of the reverend Father, Luther, from death."

Luthardt furnishes this version of the event: "Myconius, the venerated superintendent of Gotha, was in the last stage of consumption, and already speechless. Luther wrote to him that he must not die: 'May God not let me hear so long as I live that you are dead, but cause you to survive me. I pray this earnestly, and will have it granted, and my will will be granted herein, Amen.' 'I was so horrified,' said Myconius, afterwards, 'when I read what the good man had written, that it seemed to me as though I had heard Christ say, "Lazarus, come forth."' And from that time Myconius was, as it were, kept from the grave by the power of Luther's prayers, and did not die till after Luther's death." Luthardt, "Moral Truths of Christianity," p. 298.

The stout lion heart of the Reformer revolted against the grotesque miracles of Antichrist, but the believing heart of the Christian took the promises of God, and pleaded them and proved them; and he gained what he regarded as the greatest of conquests—that of having demonstrated Scripture, so as to be able to say of one text in the Bible, This I know for certain to be true."

Richard Baxter will be listened to with special deference on the question before us. He was so bold in uttering his convictions that Boyle said of him that "he feared no man's displeasure, nor hoped for any man's preferment;" and he was also so devout that Joseph Alleine was accustomed to preface his quotations from him with the words, "As most divinely saith that man of God, holy Mr. Baxter."

He wrote very decidedly in defense of present miraculous interpositions for God's faithful. Speaking of what he calls "eminent providences," he says:

"I am persuaded that there is scarcely a godly experienced Christian that carefully observeth and faithfully recordeth God's providence towards him but is able to bring forth some such experiment, and to show you some strange and unusual mercies which may plainly discover an Almighty disposer, making good the promises of this scripture to His servants; some in desperate diseases of body; some in other apparent dangers delivered so suddenly or so much against the common course of nature when all the best remedies have failed, that no second cause could have any hand in their deliverance." "Saints Rest," Part II., chap. vi., sec. 5.

After referring to some remarkable instances in the lives of the Reformers, he says:

"But why need I fetch examples so far off? or to recite the multitude of them which Church history doth afford us? Is there ever a praying Christian here who knoweth what it is importunately to strive with God, and to plead His promises with Him, believingly, that cannot give in his experiences of most remarkable answers? I know men's atheism and infidelity will never want somewhat to say against the most eminent providences, though they were miracles themselves. That nature which is so ignorant of God, and at enmity with Him, will not acknowledge Him in His clear discoveries to the world, but will ascribe all to fortune or nature, or some such idol, which, indeed, is nothing. But when mercies are granted in the very time of prayer, and that when to reason there is no hope, and that without the use or help of any other means or creature, yea, and perhaps many times over and over; is not this as plain as if God from heaven should say to us, I am fulfilling to thee the true word of my promise in Christ my Sonne? How many times have I known the prayer of faith to save the sick when all physicians have given them up as dead!"[15] "It has been my own case more than once or twice or ten times, when means have all failed, and the highest art of reason has sentenced me hopeless, yet have I been relieved by the prevalency of fervent prayer, and that (as the physician saith 'tuto, cito, et jucunde,' my flesh and my heart failed, but God is the strength of my heart and my portion forever). And though He yet keep me under necessary weakness, and wholesome sickness, and certain expectation of further necessities, and assaults, yet am I constrained, by most convincing experiences, to set up this stone of remembrance, and publickly to the praise of the Almighty, to acknowledge that certainly God is true of His promises, and that they are indeed His own infallible word, and that it is a most excellent privilege to have interest in God, and a spirit of supplication to be importunate with Him. I doubt not but most Christians that observe the spirit and providences are able to attest this prevalency of prayer by their own experiences." Ibid.

---

[15] Here Baxter subjoins a note to be given presently.

He then gives a detailed account of his own remarkable healing, which we quote in full:

"Among abundance of instances that I could give, my conscience commandeth me here to give you this one, as belonging to the very words here written. I had a tumour rise on one of the tonsils or almonds of my throat, round like a pease, and at first no bigger; and at last no bigger than a small button, and hard like a bone. The fear lest it should prove a cancer troubled me more than the thing itself. I used first dissolving medicines, and after lenient for palliation, and all in vain, for about a quarter of a year. At last my conscience smote me for silencing so many former deliverances, that I had had in answer of prayers; merely in pride, lest I should be derided as making ostentation of God's special mercies to myself, as if I were a special favourite of heaven, I had made no public mention of them: I was that morning to preach just what is here written, and in obedience to my conscience, I spoke these words which are now in this page:—viz., 'How many times have I known the prayer of faith to save the sick when all physicians have given them up as dead'—with some enlargements not here written. When I went to church I had my tumour as before (for I frequently saw it in the glasse, and felt it constantly). As soon as I had done preaching, I felt it was gone, and hasting to the glasse, I saw that there was not the least vestigium or cicatrix, or mark wherever it had been: nor did I at all discern what became of it. I am sure I neither swallowed it nor spit it out, and it was unlikely to dissolve by any natural cause, that had been hard like a bone a quarter of a year, notwithstanding all dissolving gargarismes. I thought fit to mention this, because it was done just as I spoke the words here written in this page. Many such marvellous mercies I have received, and known that others have received in answer to prayers." Ibid.

At once we imagine the explanations which will be given to this artlessly narrated incident. We do not vouch for its supernatural character. We have introduced it simply to show that Richard Baxter believed in modern miracles of healing, and there we leave it. It is not the authenticity of the wonder but the opinion of the man which we wish now to establish. That must be considered unquestionable.

John Albert Bengel is not only greatly esteemed but held in real affection by lovers of God's word who have studied his commentary. He expounds pithily, but what is far better, he believes intensely. "His works," says Dorner, "were the first cockcrowing of that new kind of exegesis which the Church so much needed." His is preeminently the exegesis of faith in distinction from the exegesis of reason. If he finds things in the Bible too hard for his critical faculty, he finds nothing too hard for his believing faculty. Hence his interpretations are not a sizing and sorting of Scripture to the dimensions of human experience, but a frank acceptance of it as God's truth. The word never appears shrunken as it comes forth from his hand; it does not present a scant weight, as though it had paid toll to modern doubt. "Faith takes up all she can get and marches bravely onward," is a saying of his that describes better than any other his conduct in handling Scripture. Now, by faith Bengel staggered not at the promise of miraculous healing, which he found in the New Testament, but believed it, and confessed it, and rejoiced in it. In speaking of the gift of healing he says:

"It seems to have been given by God that it might always remain in the Church as a specimen of the other gifts: just as the portion of manna betokened the ancient miracles." Comment on James 5:17. "O happy simplicity interrupted or lost through unbelief," he exclaims. And yet he declares, "even in our day faith has in every believer a hidden miraculous power. Every result of prayer is really miraculous, even though this be not apparent; although in many, because of their own weakness and the world's unworthiness—not merely because the church once planted needs not miracles (though no doubt the early New Testament miracles have made for the Lord an everlasting name)—that power does not exert itself in our day. Signs were in the beginning the props of faith: now they are the object of faith." On Mark 16:14.

And then, for confirming his assertions of his belief in the possibility of modern miracles, he introduces the following instance: At Leonberg, a town of Wurtemberg, A.D. 1644, thirteenth Sunday after Trinity, a girl of twenty-three years of age was so disabled in her limbs as hardly to be able to creep along by the help of crutches. But whilst the Dean, Raumier was his name, was from the pulpit dwelling on the miraculous power of Jesu's name, she suddenly was raised up and restored to the use of her limbs."

This story the American editor omits, as though solicitous for the critic's reputation; but Faucett, the English translator, retains it in its place, and adds from information gathered from other sources that "this happened in the presence of the Duke of Eberhard and his courtiers, and was committed to the public records, which are above all suspicion."

Edward Irving is another illustrious confessor bearing witness to the doctrine we are defending. A man of wonderful endowments,[16] his highest gift seems to have been that of faith. He believed, with the whole strength and intensity of his nature, everything which he found written in the Scriptures. Cast upon times of great spiritual deadness, he longed to see Christendom mightily revived, and he conceived that this could only be effected by stirring up the Church to recover her forfeited endowments. "To restore is to revive" was emphatically his motto. He gave great offence by his utterances, and had his name cast out as evil. He was accused of offering strange fire upon the altar of his Church, because he thought to relight the fire of Pentecost. Need enough was there of restoration,

---

[16] "But I hold withal, and not the less firmly for these discrepancies in our moods and judgments, that Edward Irving possesses more of the spirit and purpose of the first Reformers, that he has more of the head and heart, the life and unction and the genial power of Martin Luther, than any man now alive: yea, than any man of this or the last century. I see in Edward Irving a minister of Christ after the order of Paul."—Coleridge, "Works," V. vi., p. 115.

when teachers had so far made void the Word of God by their traditions that in their discussion with him they openly appealed from the Bible to the standards. Have you never read what Jehoiakim the son of Judah did with his penknife upon the prophet's roll?—how "it came to pass that when Jehudi had read three or four leaves, he cut it with his penknife and cast it into the fire!" Alas that modern theology should have given occasion to be accused of doing likewise with 1 Corinthians 12 and sundry other parts of Scripture that tell about "to another the gift of healing by the same Spirit, and another the working of miracles, to another prophecy," etc.

Irving, with a zeal for the Lord not always temperate, accused the Church of having clipped out these portions from the Scripture with her exegetical penknife, because she had said, "These things do not pertain to the Church of today." And he went farther—"The Lord commanded Jeremiah to take another roll and to write in it all the former words that were in the first roll which Jehoiakim the son of Judah had burned." And Irving conceived that he had a similar commission, or at least permission,—not to make any new revelation, as he was accused,—but to retrace the faded lines of the old, wherein it spoke of "spiritual gifts": and so he encouraged his flock to seek for, and if the Lord should permit, to exercise, the gifts of prophecy and of healing. This was his chief affront, and that which brought his splendid career under an eclipse,—a result inevitable, indeed, considering that he was to be judged by those who knew no distinction between innovation and renovation.

But bating any extravagances into which he may have fallen, we confess that our heart has always gone out to him in reverence for his heroic fidelity to the Word of God, and his willingness, in allegiance to that Word, to follow Christ "without the camp bearing the reproach." And we believe that when the Master shall come to recompense His servants, this one will attain a high reward and receive of the Lord double for the broken heart with which he went down to his grave.

Irving wrote upon this subject with his usual masterly ability. Considering the Church to be "the Body of Christ," and the endowment of the Church to be "the fulness of Him that filleth all in all," he held that the Church ought to exhibit in every age something of that miraculous power which belongs to the Head. That as she endures hardness and humiliation as united to Him who was on the cross, so she should exhibit something of supernatural energy as united with Him who is on the throne. This he conceived to be essential for the Church's full witness to Christ—to Him "who is now creation's scepter-bearer as He was heretofore creation's burden-bearer."

He lamented that the Church in her working has descended so much to the plane of the merely natural—that in preaching the arts of the logician and the rhetorician have so far supplanted the gifts of the Spirit. "The power of miracles must either be speedily revived in the Church," he says, "or there will be a universal dominion of the mechanical philosophy, and faith will be fairly expelled to give place to the law of cause and effect acting and ruling in the world of mind as it doth in the world of sense." "Works," V., 479.

He considered miracles to be intended not only for a perpetual demonstration of Christ's power as now living and glorified, but also as a visible foretoken of His coming kingdom. He has pointed out with marked clearness the significance of the various signs promised in the great commission, showing how these were given as firstfruits of the kingdom of God as it shall appear in its full consummation. As that kingdom was always to be preached, he held that these signs were promised as the perpetual accompaniment of that preaching. He concluded that their withdrawal is due to the Church's unfaithfulness, and not to any revocation on the part of God.

"These gifts have ceased, I would say, just as the verdure and leaves and flowers and fruits of the spring and summer and autumn cease in winter: because by the chill and wintry blasts which have blown over the Church, her power to put forth her glorious beauty hath been prevented. But because the winter is without a green leaf or beautiful flower, do men thereof argue that there shall be flowers and fruits no more?

"Trusting in the word of God, who hath created everything to produce and bring forth its kind, man puts out his hand in winter and makes preparations for the coming year: so if the Church be still in existence, and that no one denies—and if it be the law and end of her being to embody a firstfruit and earnest of the power which Christ is to put forth in the redemption of all nature—then, what though she hath been brought so low, her life is still in her, and that life will under a more genial day put forth its native powers." "The Church with her Endowment of Holiness and Power."—"Works," V., p., 101.

It was from such convictions as these that he reasoned so powerfully and prayed so earnestly for the recovery by the Church of her primitive gifts. If the effort brought pain and persecution to him, we believe it has brought forth some very sweet and genial fruits in others. He was no mere theorist. He not only exhorted his flock "to live by faith continually on Jesus for the body as well as the soul," but he has told us the story of his casting himself on the Lord when mighty disease laid hold of him; and how his faith was tried to the last extremity, till with swimming brain and deathly sweat he stood holding on to the sides of the pulpit, waiting for God to fulfil in the eyes of the people His word, "The prayer of faith shall save the sick;" and how his Redeemer at last appeared for his help and loosed for him the bands of sickness, enabling him to preach on that morning with such demonstration and power of the Spirit as he had rarely known.

Thomas Erskine has written on this subject with rare insight and depth of conviction. Those who have read his writings know what a subtle and intuitive spiritual apprehension he had. A barrister by profession, he is far more widely known as a theologian, while he is most deeply revered as a Christian, "who," to use Dr. Hanna's words in his preface to his Letters, "moved so lovingly and attractively among his fellow-men and who walked so closely and constantly with God."

Speaking of miraculous healing and the other gifts, he says: "But I still continue to think, that to any one whose expectations are formed by and founded on the New Testament, the disappearance of these gifts from the Church must be a far greater difficulty than their reappearance could possibly be." "Letters," p. 408.

In his correspondence with Dr. Chalmers, when the latter argued that we ought not to desire signs from the Lord, but to be satisfied with the ordinary manifestations of the Spirit, he replied that we ought to desire them, if God has ordained them: "If the Lord gives these things as means, surely it is not genuine humility which says, 'I am satisfied without them.' When the Lord desired Ahaz to ask a sign he answered, 'I will not ask, neither will I tempt the Lord:' but he is severely rebuked for this apparent humility." (Isa. 7:12, 13.)

His strong conviction was that the miraculous gifts were designed to be a permanent endowment of the Church: "The great and common mistake with regard to the gifts is that they were intended merely to authenticate or to witness to the inspiration of the canon of Scripture, and that therefore when the canon was completed they should cease: whereas they were intended to witness to the exaltation of Christ as the Head of the body, the Church. Had the faith of the Church continued pure and full, these gifts of the Spirit would never have disappeared. There is no revocation by Christ of that word." "Brazen Serpent," p. 203; Id., p. 198. Mark 16:17, 18.

With such views he watched with great interest any indications of a revival of these gifts, and in the movement in that direction going on in his day he believed he witnessed some genuine instances of miraculous healing, as well as of speaking with tongues. We refer to one case mentioned in his Letters: "In March 1830, in the town of Port Glasgow, on the Clyde, lived a family of MacDonalds, twin brothers, James and George, with their sisters. One of the sisters, Margaret, of saintly life, lay very ill, and apparently nigh to death. She had received a remarkable baptism of the Spirit on her sick bed, and had been praying for her brothers that they might be anointed in like manner. One day, when James was standing by, and she was interceding that he might at that time be endowed with the power of the Holy Ghost, the Spirit came upon him with marvelous manifestations. His whole countenance was lighted up, and with a step and manner of most indescribable majesty he walked up to Margaret's bedside and addressed her in these words: 'Arise and stand upright.' He repeated the words, took her by the hand, and she arose. Her recovery was instantaneous and complete, and the report of it produced a profound sensation, and many came from great distances to sec her. Mr. Erskine visited the house and made careful and prolonged inquiry into the facts, and put on record his conviction of the genuineness of the miracle." "Letters," pp. 176, 182, 183.

His whole discussion of the subject in the work referred to, "The Brazen Serpent," is deeply instructive, and especially his exposition of the intention and significance of miracles of healing as signs.

Dr. Horace Bushnell, in his well-known work "Nature and the Supernatural," not only admits the existence of present-day miracles, but considers that a denial of their possibility would imperil his whole argument for the supernatural. Conceding that the Church as a whole has lost her miraculous faith, and would be inclined to repel it were it offered to her, and admitting that thinking men are not open to conviction on this point, because "the human mind, as educated mind, is just now at the point of religious apogee, where it is occupied or preoccupied by nature, and cannot think it rational to suppose that God does anything longer which exceeds the casualties of nature," he yet holds that among humble and simple-hearted believers "sporadic cases" of miracles have constantly appeared, and continue to appear. And not only this: he considers that in our time there are signs of a revival of the primitive apostolic gifts; that Christians "feeling after some way out of the dulness of second-hand faith, and the dryness of merely reasoned gospel, are longing for a kind of faith that shows God in living commerce with men such as He vouchsafed them in former times." "Probably, therefore," he continues, "there may just now be coming forth a more distinct and widely attested dispensation of gifts and miracles than has been witnessed for centuries."

Dr. Bushnell's testimony as a whole is quite remarkable, because it is that of a cultivated reasoner looking at the question through the eyes of logic, as well as through the eyes of faith. His well-argued discussion and wide array of facts ought at least to arrest the attention of the savants who toss off this subject with a derisive sneer. That unripe scepticism, which denies before it has even doubted, has nowhere been more arrogant than on this field. Presumptuous enough it is to attempt to pick a miracle to pieces with the steel fingers of logic, but to leave it coolly alone is worse. And yet this is the method which reason has too often taken with anything professedly supernatural in these days. Scientific reason and Christian reason have passed by modern miracles as poor relations, to be looked at askance but not to be admitted into the best circles of faith and credence. And it is, therefore, quite gratifying to note the frank and cordial recognition which a thinker like Dr. Bushnell extends to them. Healing, prophecy, and gifts of tongues he admits as possible, and to some extent operative today as in the beginning. From a large array of instances adduced in his work we give place to but one, referring the reader for further information to the fourteenth chapter of the work named, in which he discusses the proposition: "Miracles and supernatural gifts not discontinued."

The case cited is from the experience of a friend of his, who had been healed by prayer himself, and had, as he believed, received the gift of healing. He gives the instance to Dr. Bushnell in writing, and the doctor considers his character and veracity to be such as to put his story beyond question:

"At length one of his children, whom he had with him away from home, was taken ill with scarlet fever. And now the question was (I give his own words), 'What was to be done? The Lord had healed my own sickness, but would He heal my son? I conferred with a brother in the Lord, who, having no faith in Christ's healing power, urged me to send instantly for the doctor, and I despatched his groom on horseback to fetch him. Before the doctor arrived my mind was filled with revelation on the subject. I saw that I had fallen into a snare by turning away from the Lord's healing hand to lean on medical skill. I felt grievously condemned in my conscience; a fear also fell on me that if I persevered in my unbelieving course my son would die, as his oldest brother had. The symptoms in both were precisely similar. The doctor arrived. My son, he said, was suffering from a scarlet fever, and medicine should be sent immediately. While he stood prescribing I resolved to withdraw the child and cast him on the Lord. And when he was gone I called the nurse and told her to take the child into the nursery and lay him on the bed. I then fell on my knees, confessing the sin I had committed against the Lord's healing power. I also prayed most earnestly that it would please my heavenly Father to forgive my sin, and to show that He forgave it by causing the fever to be rebuked. I received a mighty conviction that my prayer was heard, and I arose and went to the nursery, at the end of a long passage, to see what the Lord had done; and on opening the door, to my astonishment, the boy was sitting up in his bed, and on seeing me cried out, "I am quite well and want to have my dinner." In an hour he was dressed, and well, and eating his dinner, and when the physic arrived it was cast out of the window.

"Next morning the doctor returned, and on meeting me at the garden gate he said, "I hope your son is no worse?" "He is very well, I thank you," said I in reply. "What can you mean?" rejoined the doctor. "I will tell you; come in and sit down." I then told him all that had occurred, at which he fairly gasped with surprise. "May I see your son?" he asked. "Certainly, doctor; but I see that you do not believe me." We proceeded upstairs, and my son was playing with his brother on the floor. The doctor felt his pulse, and said, "Yes, the fever is gone." Finding also a fine, healthy surface on his tongue, he added, "Yes, he is quite well; I suppose it was the crisis of his disease."'" "Nature and the Supernatural," p. 480.

These testimonies might be increased by the addition of such names as those of Hugh Grotius, the Dutch theologian, and Lavater, "the Fenelon of Switzerland," as he has been called, and Hugh McNeil, the eminent English evangelical minister of the last generation, and Thomas Boys, M.A., of Trinity College, Cambridge, and others.[17]

---

[17] The works of Thomas Boys, "The Christian Dispensation Miraculous," and "Proofs of Miraculous Faith and Experience of the Church in all Ages," are full of learning and information on this whole subject, and this book gratefully acknowledges its

But we have not space to refer to more. These are a goodly array of witnesses; yet not because of their eminence have we summoned them. We care little for the testimony of a deep thinker except he has thought deeply and devoutly upon the subject in hand. The shorter sounding line, if it has dropped its lead to the utmost limit, has told us more of the depth than the longer one that remained coiled and dry. And so the very mediocre theologian who has studied this question to the extent of his capacity is a better witness than the most profound who has never investigated it, but has rested in unreasoning assent to what Dr. Bushnell calls "the clumsy assumption" that all miracles closed with the apostolic age.

---

indebtedness to them for several quotations and translations from rare and inaccessible works.

# Chapter 6
# THE TESTIMONY OF MISSIONS

There is a special and weighty reason why we should lay emphasis on any testimonies on this subject coming from those who are preaching the Gospel among the Pagans. The rigid logic which is supposed to fence out miracles from modern Christendom does not seem to have been careful to include heathendom in its prohibition. For when it is said that "miracles belong to the planting of Christianity, not to its progress and development," it will at once strike us that missions are practically the planting of Christianity. There is really little if any difference between Paul at Melita and Judson in India. In each instance it is the herald of the Gospel set down among a superstitious and idolatrous people. And admitting the proposition just quoted to be true, it would be very difficult to say why, if Paul went into the house of Publius in the one place and laid his hands on his sick father and healed him, it might not be permitted Judson to go into some home in Burmah and do the same. And if it be said that signs are not needed while we have the history of the Christian Church, and the influence of powerful Christian nations for the authentication and enforcement of the Gospel,[18] it must still be remembered that these forces are practically powerless until by the planting of Christianity the heathen have been made acquainted with ecclesiastical history and brought in contact with Christian civilization; so that the argument comes back again to this conclusion,—that if miracles belong to the planting of Christianity, there would be no inherent improbability of their appearing on missionary fields, and among those who are engaged in introducing the Gospel into new countries. The justness of this conclusion has been recognized by several writers.

We are glad to find, for example, so devout and eminent a theologian as Professor Christlieb of Bonn accepting most candidly and frankly this position. For after admitting the force of the argument against miracles in Christianized countries he says:

"Our age, however, is still characterized by the establishment of new Churches. The work of missions is outwardly at least more extended than it ever was before. In this region, therefore, according to our former rule, miracles should not be entirely wanting.[19] Nor are they. We cannot therefore fully admit the proposition that no more miracles are performed in our day. In the history of modern missions we find many wonderful occurrences which unmistakably remind us of the apostolic age. In both periods there are similar hindrances to be

---

[18] see Alford on Mark 16

[19] Abp. Tillotson puts forth a similar view. "Works," x., p. 230.

overcome in the heathen world, and similar confirmations of the word are needed to convince the dull sense of men: we may therefore expect miracles in this case." "Modern Doubt and Christian Belief," p. 332.

And then, as though less afraid of the imputation of credulity than of scepticism, he gives several instances, in the genuineness of which he expresses entire confidence. These we believe are but samples of hundreds that might be produced were it not for the exceeding timidity, the shyness, amounting almost to shamefacedness, with which so many Christians approach this subject. Of course, with this sentiment of distrust generally prevailing on the subject, we could hardly expect that witnesses would be very forward in reporting things indiscreetly supernatural, though quite confident of having seen them.

We venture, however, to give several instances of what seem to be divine healing, as they have been reported from missionary fields—the first three being those cited by Dr. Christlieb in the work just referred to:

"And now read the history of Hans Egede, the first evangelical missionary in Greenland. He had given the Esquimaux a pictorial representation of the miracles of Christ before he had mastered their language. His hearers, who, like many in the time of Christ, had a perception only for bodily relief, urge him to prove the power of this Redeemer of the world upon their sick people. With many sighs and prayers he ventures to lay his hands upon several, prays over them, and lo, he makes them whole in the name of Jesus Christ! The Lord could not reveal Himself plainly enough to this mentally blunted and degraded race by merely spiritual means, and therefore bodily signs were needed."

"At a Rhenish mission station in South Africa, in 1858, an earnest native Christian saw an old friend who had become lame in both legs. Impressed with a peculiar sense of believing confidence, he went into the bushes to pray, and then came straight up to the cripple, and said, 'The same Jesus who made the lame to walk can do so still: I say to thee, in the name of Jesus, rise and walk!' The lame man, with kindred faith, raised himself on his staff and walked, to the astonishment of all who knew him."—Vide the "Memoire of Kleinschmidt," Barmen, 1866, p. 58, ff.

Another most remarkable instance occurred in the case of a missionary of the Rhenish society, named Nommensen, working in Sumatra:

"On one occasion a heathen who had designs on his life managed secretly to mix a deadly poison in the rice which Nommensen was preparing for his dinner. Without suspicion the missionary ate the rice, and the heathen watched for him to fall down dead. Instead of this, however, the promise contained in Mark 16:18 was fulfilled, and he did not experience the slightest inconvenience. The heathen, by this palpable miraculous proof of the Christian God's power, became convinced of the truth, and was eventually converted; but not until his conscience had impelled him to confess his guilt to Nommensen did the latter know from what danger he had been preserved. This incident is well attested, and the missionary still lives."—1873, (vd. v, "Rohden Geschichte der Rhein," Missionsgesellsschaft, p. 324.)

It will be seen that these instances cover several specifications in Mark 16:17, 18. Their miraculous character cannot of course be vouched for with certainty. For we have not witnesses supernaturally inspired to accredit works supernaturally wrought, if there are such still. But one would hardly wish to charge deception on those who have reported them. For us, however, their probability rests more strongly on the words of the great commission under which these missionaries were acting than on the trustworthiness of human testimony.[20]

Doctrines which have been almost universally denied are certain to force themselves into acceptance again if they are in the Bible, and that Bible is studied. And a promise in the missionary's commission which says, "These signs shall follow," is liable now and then to break through custom and prejudice and get itself fulfilled. Besides, that commission is certain to fall into the hands of native preachers, who are unskilled in the arts of refining and spiritualizing Scripture, and who know no better than to take God literally at His word. And who can tell what may not happen when a Christian who has not learned to doubt comes to God to claim the fulfilment of one of His promises? In such a case we may hear of miracles quite artless and rude in their form.

A missionary of the Presbyterian Board who has been laboring for many years in China declares that with the New Testament in their hands the native Christians are constantly finding and putting in practice the promises for miraculous healing. This fact has led him to a careful revision of his opinions on the subject. He writes:

"Fully believing that the gifts of the Spirit were not to be taken from the Church, I feel assured that our faith ought to exercise and claim their use now. The salvation aimed for by all should be present release from sin and the power of Satan. If this is attained, then the whole advantage of Christ's life, death, and resurrection will be secured. Healing is as much a part of this as any verbal proclamation of the good news. The ministry of healing, therefore, cannot be divorced from the duty of the missionary."

An honored missionary among the Karens gives the following experience:

"While traveling in the Pegu district I was strongly urged to visit an out-of-the-way village, in which were only a few Christians. Entering the house of one of

---

[20] "But, inasmuch as far later times are full of testimonies to this point, I know not from what motive some persons restrain the gift to the first ages. While I readily grant to such persons that there was a richer abundance of miracles in order that the foundation of so great a structure might, in spite of the world's power, be laid, I cannot with them perceive why we should believe that this promise of Christ has ceased to be in force. Wherefore, if any one preach Christ, as He would have Himself preached to the nations that know Him not (for miracles are peculiarly intended for such, 1 Cor. 14:22), I doubt not that the promise will still be found to stand good; for the gifts of God are without repentance (Rom. 11:29). But we, whenever the fault lies in our own sloth or unbelief, throw the blame on Him." Hugh Grotius, 1583-1645.

them, I had been seated but a little while when there came in a Karen, an entire stranger, but whose salutation proved him a Christian. He at once said that, hearing that the teacher had come to visit the village, he came to beg that I would go and pray for his son who was very ill—he feared dying. He quoted James 5:14, 15 as his excuse. Of course Mrs.—and myself went at once, accompanied by the three or four Christians of the house in which we were. The patient was found to be a child of about fifteen years of age, possibly not over fourteen, but through scrofula he was distorted and crippled so that he could not walk, indeed had never walked upright, but crept painfully on knees and hands. He was greatly wasted, and had been much worse for some weeks, and at the time was perfectly helpless through extreme weakness. He had every appearance of one near death. We prayed, each in turn, the lad mingling short requests with ours. I think in all seven brethren offered petitions. A little bottle of medicine was left from our scanty supplies, and we took leave of the poor little fellow. Six months afterwards the father came to the city, and on inquiring of him he said that his son was well,—well as he had never been in his life, and was actually walking on his feet; that the heathen families living in the village were deeply impressed, and said unhesitatingly that our prayers had saved him. I asked him his own opinion. He most emphatically, in his strong Karen way, said: God has done it; God has healed him.' He then said, Teacher; this is no new thing; I was with your father-in-law many times when God, in answer to prayers, healed the sick, and that is why I asked you to pray with my boy, and now he is healed.'"

Many testimonies have been recently published by missionaries of their own recovery from hopeless sickness through the prayers of faith. We can give place to but one, and that quite abridged in form. It is from Rev. Albert Norton, and is written to Dr. Stanton of Cincinnati, formerly moderator of the General Assembly. After describing his terrible sickness in Elichpoor, India, June 1879—an abscess in the liver which had worked itself through the pleura and was discharging itself into the right lung—the most intense pain ever endured, and withal malarious remittent fever, etc., he continues:

"I was thinking only of how I might die as easy as possible, when I was aroused by strong desire to live for my family, and to preach the unsearchable riches of the Gospel, and the thought came, 'Why cannot God heal you?' My dear wife was the only Christian believer, except an ignorant Kerkoo lad, within eighteen miles. At my request she anointed me with oil, and united her prayers with mine that God might at once heal me. While I was praying vocally, before I felt any change in my body, I felt perfectly certain that God had heard and answered our prayers. When we were through praying we commenced praising; for the acute pain in my right side and the fever had left me. I was able at once to read from the Bible, and to look out some passages from the Greek Testament. Neither the fever nor the acute pain returned, and from that hour I began rapidly to grow stronger. In a few days I was able to walk half a mile without fatigue. In this sickness I took no medicine, and had the help of no physician but Jesus. To him be all the praise and glory. Why should it be thought a strange thing that He can heal our bodies? It is written of Him, 'Himself took our infirmities and bare our sicknesses.' Is it not said of our Lord, 'Who healeth all thy diseases,' as well as 'Who forgiveth all thine iniquities'?" "The Great Physician," by Rev. W. E. Boardman.

We must believe, however, that if God really stretched forth His hand to heal in these instances, it was for the furtherance of the Gospel as the chief purpose. Miracles are the signs and not the substance of Christianity. They are for the confirmation of the Word, and not merely for the comfort of the body. And this fact especially enhances the probability that they might not be entirely wanting in heathen lands.

The blind man must read his Bible by means of raised letters and through the coarser sense of touch, since he is lacking in eyesight. And what if, to the blind pagans, God should be pleased now and then to present the Gospel embossed in signs and wonders, if "haply they might feel after Him and find Him," in this way, when they could not at first discern Him with the spiritual understanding? No more serious objection could be made against this method than that it is a revival of the primitive,—"And they went forth and preached everywhere, the Lord working with them, and confirming the words with signs following." Not for the satisfaction of the flesh but for the glory of God and the vindication of His truth does our Lord stretch out His healing hand and "make bare His holy arm in the eyes of all the nations." If it should be His good pleasure to make use of those other miracles, the miracles of martyrdom, and to show the power of His grace in the supernatural endurance of His servants under suffering, the same end has been reached. Perpetua and Felicitas, going to a terrible death with a serenity rising into absolute joy—the declaration of utter insensibility to pain made before a multitude of witnesses—who has not read of the thrilling impression thus produced upon the heathen, and of the irresistible impulse thereby given to the truth? These are but miracles of healing seen on their reverse side; the Lord's hand stretched out to rob death of its pain, instead of robbing death of its victim.[21] "That the word of the Lord may have free course and be glorified whether by my life or by my death," whether by my cure or by my patience under suffering,—this must be our prayer always. But God be praised that He wills the health of His people and not their hurt. The priests of Baal seek to prove their God by cutting themselves with knives and lancets. Elijah has just proved his God by calling the widow's dead son to life and delivering him to his mother. How greatly do the idolaters, with their endless worship of self-torture, need to be taught this truth: that our God is one that makes alive and not one that kills.

Would, then, that the heathen could know Christ as the Healer! Who has not said it as he has read of the awful loathsomeness of their sicknesses and the cruel impositions of their doctors. Next to the intolerable tyranny of evil priests is that

---

[21] "Martyrdoms I reckon amongst miracles, because they exceed the strength of human nature." Bacon.

of "the forgers of lies, the physicians of no value," with which every pagan nation is afflicted. Can we describe or imagine the joy of the heathen's deliverance from the hopeless search for peace of conscience, as he finds Christ, the Sin-Pardoner? "Great Spirit, untie the load of our sins. If this load were bound round our shoulders we could untie it for ourselves; but it is bound round our hearts, and we cannot untie it, but Thou canst. Lord, untie it now." So prayed a poor Fiji Islander. "Journal of Wesleyan Missions." Was not the revelation beyond all price that made known to him the fact that Christ "bore our sins in His own body on the tree," and so could instantly lift the load which he had toiled in vain to lift? And what if added to this he could hear and appropriate that other revelation, that "Himself bare our sickness"? If when "the whole head is sick and the whole heart faint, from the sole of the foot even unto the head, no soundness in it, but wounds and bruises and putrefying sores"; and if, after spending all his living on false physicians, his wounds "have not been closed, neither bound up, neither mollified with ointment," he could then know the Savior's healing touch laid upon him, and bear the word, "Thou art made whole," what glory would he give to our Lord and Redeemer!

Is it unbecoming or presumptuous for us to conjecture what effects would ensue if the Gospel were thus to be preached on heathen fields "with signs following"? Sickness is the dark shadow of sin, and nowhere does it lie so heavily as on the pagan nations. If now and then that shadow were seen to be lifted by the Lord's hand, the event could hardly fail to open a wide and effectual door of entrance for the Gospel. God forbid that we should desire or grasp for anything which it is not His pleasure to give! But what if it should seem to us that the great commission demands these signs instead of forbidding them? Baptism, that sign of Christ's death and resurrection and of our justification thereby, is in the commission: and what bitter battles have been fought in the Church for its maintenance! And healing the sick, that sign of Christ glorified and alive forevermore, is in the commission just as unequivocally. And yet we are so weak and perplexed and impotent before it. Yes! it is there: but "who is sufficient for these things?" Who of us would quite dare to repeat on behalf of our missionary brethren, some of whom are laboring among hostile rulers and bloodthirsty tribes, the apostle's prayer—"And now, Lord, behold their threatenings and grant unto Thy servants that with all boldness they may speak Thy word, by stretching forth Thine hand to heal: and that signs and wonders may be done in the name of Thy holy Child Jesus"? If we cannot utter this prayer we may at least join in the petition which a devout commentator breathes over the closing words of Mark's Gospel: "Let us cry to the Lord, Strengthen and bless the hands of Your authenticated messengers: that they may rightly lay them upon men; and that before Your coming again Your promise may be abundantly fulfilled: they shall be healed: it shall be well with them." Stier's "Words of Jesus."

# Chapter 7

# THE TESTIMONY OF THE ADVERSARY

His testimony ought not to be cited, it will be said, since he is "a liar and the father of it."

But if we bear in mind always who and what he is, his witness may serve a very excellent end. For we must know, unless we are utterly "ignorant of his devices," that his deceptions are generally counterfeits of Divine realities. His business is to resist the Almighty by mimicking His words and His works. Hence his lies are often very serviceable as the negatives from which to reproduce photographs of God's truths. And if we will notice what the adversary is especially busy in bringing forward at any period, we may by contrast infer what vital doctrine or important truth of God is struggling into recognition.

We regard this principle as so unquestionable, and so distinctly scriptural, that we are always surprised to see Christian writers betrayed by overlooking it. "If you credit any modern miracles in God's true Church, you must logically concede the genuineness of the alleged miracles of the apostate church," it is often confidently said. Nay! but have you never read of him "whose coming is after the working of Satan with all power and signs and lying wonders"? 2 Thess. 2:10, 12. Also, Rev. 16:14, "Spirits of devils working miracles." The working of Antichrist is the counterpart of the working of Christ. Not feeble, transparently false, and contemptible are the miracles of the adversary. "Signs and wonders" are predicted of him—the same terms as those applied to the works of Christ. And not only that, but "all power" is ascribed to him—the same words employed which Christ used at His ascension, when laying claim to universal authority. Without stopping to consider what limitations the language may have in such connection, its use is certainly startling, and indicates that the miracles of Antichrist are likely to be powerful and impressive, and fitted to "deceive the very elect." But it is most illogical to conclude that we must believe in lying wonders, because we believe in real wonders; and that we must credit the miracles of the apostate Church because we find those which we credit in the true Church. We say "miracles of the apostate Church." The Fathers and the Reformers attributed actual miracles to Antichrist,—wonders of a super-human character, only demoniacal instead of divine, wrought through the agency of evil spirits to simulate the works of the Spirit of God.[22] And this view seems scriptural. In

---

[22] Augustine declares that miracles may emanate "either from seducing spirits or from God Himself." Huss says, "The disciples of Antichrist are more distinguished by miracles than those of Christ, and will be so in days to come." Defence of Wickliffe," p. 115. Calvin says, "Satan perverts the things which otherwise are truly works of God, and mis-employs miracles to obscure God's glory." Comment on 2 Thess. 2:9.

describing the perils of the last days Paul declares concerning false teachers that "as Jannes and Jambes withstood Moses, so do these also resist the truth." The method of resistance which these magicians offered, it will be remembered, was to reproduce the miracles of God's servants. When Aaron wrought wonders with his rod, "they also did in like manner with their enchantments." Miracle was matched by miracle, and wonder by wonder, up to the point where God triumphed by confounding the deceivers.

So has it been with the Church of Christ all through her history. Satan has ever been seeking to thwart God by imitation rather than by denial. And we imagine that he has done more for building up his kingdom through the apostate miracle-mongers who have claimed Divine power than through the infidel miracle-deniers who have disputed it. But there have been nevertheless certain evident tokens of spuriousness attaching to apostate miracles that have indicated their true character to believers. There is a kind of Egyptian crudeness about them which suggests the art of the sorcerer rather than the touch of God's finger. Alleged healing by contact with the bones of dead saints; pains assuaged by making the sign of the cross over the sufferer; recoveries effected by pilgrimages to the shrines of martyrs, and evil spirits exorcized by the crucifix or the image of the Virgin! who does not see the vast contrast in these methods from the dignified and simple methods of Christ and His apostles? "God never puts a man upon the stage that Satan does not immediately bring forward an ape," says Godet. He will approach as near the truth as possible, and still keep to his lie. He will give us miracles through his false prophets that seem Divine in their end and purpose, but will always be careful to link them to some deadly superstition or fatal heresy.

We emphasize the assertion, therefore, that false miracles are a testimony to the existence somewhere of the true, and that we ought to be very careful lest in our revolt from the caricature, we swing over to a denial of the genuine. "According to all evidence of Scripture there never were spurious miracles without the genuine: there never were those from beneath without those from above at the same time. And prophecy agrees with fact. As tokens of the last day our Lord foretells the signs and wonders of false Christs and prophets, and Joel foretells true ones. Thus every counterfeit implies something counterfeited; and if you prove counterfeit miracles, you only tell us to open our eyes the wider and look for the originals." Rev. Thomas Boys, "Proofs of Miraculous Faith and Experience of the Church," pp. 11, 12.

In our own time we have witnessed an extraordinary forth-putting of Satanic energy in the works of modern spiritualism. This is a system more versatile in uncleanness, more fertile in blasphemy, and more prolific of adulteries, fleshly and spiritual, than any probably that has appeared for many generations. In all its acts and exhibitions it is so redolent of the foul smoke of Gehenna, that it would seem impossible that any Christian could be deceived by it; yet it has taken thousands of professed disciples of Christ captive, so that they have "gone in the way of Cain, and run greedily after the error of Balaam for reward, and perished in the gainsaying of Core." Its manifestations are characterized by just those impish grotesque and fantastic exhibitions which always distinguish the devil's works from those of Christ. Its rappings and table-tippings and materializations, and communions with the dead,—what evident tokens of perdition these should be to one who has been at all accustomed to discriminate between Divine and Satanic traits! And yet, as a competent writer declares, these things are unblushingly and openly professed and practised by Christian men in all lands: those who believe them to be really spiritual, affirming that they are wrought by good spirits; and those who disbelieve them to be the work of spirits at all, playing with them in their unbelief." Alas that such a system should be able to boast of its millions of adherents, and that in those millions thousands should be found who have borne or still bear the name of Christ! Looking at the matter in the light of Scripture, we know of no more conspicuous sign of the last days and of the "perilous times" therein predicted than this." "Whenever these things have appeared it was a sign of approaching doom. When the Canaanites practiced them the measure of their iniquity was full. When Saul applied to the witch of Endor his end was near. When these things prevailed among the Jews their day was closing. Let us not permit such among us, lest it should become the sign to us of declension and doom." Tract, What is Mesmerism? (Bosworth and Harrison.)

Now it is well known that one of the loudest pretensions of spiritualism is the claim to effect miraculous healing. It declares that Christ wrought His cures through the agency of spirits, and that it can do the same. Hence the legion of "healing mediums," and the innumerable "lying wonders " by which their assumptions are enforced.

It is very natural that decent Christians, in their recoil from such revolting wonder-working, should take the position of stout denial of all miraculous interventions in modern times, and of any supernatural healing. But we believe this to be an unworthy and unfaithful attitude. It is as though Moses and Aaron had retreated in disgust before Jannes and Jambres, instead of pressing on with miracle upon miracle till they had compelled them to surrender to the Lord of hosts. It is as though Paul had been ashamed of the power of the Spirit that was in him when he met the "damsel possessed with a spirit of divination," and had renounced his miraculous gifts for fear of being identified with soothsayers and necromancers, instead of asserting his power as he did the more mightily, and saying to the evil spirit that possessed her, "I command thee in the name of the Lord Jesus to come out of her."

It is a curious fact that in the New Testament Greek the term for sorcery is the same as that for drugs. For example, Rev. 22:15 "Without are dogs and sorcerers" (pharmacists); and Gal. 6:19 "The works of the flesh are adultery, uncleanness, lasciviousness, idolatry, witchcraft" (pharmacy). And when we think of the legion of medicine-men and medicine-women who prey upon the sick; the spiritualists and trance-doctors with their prescriptions dictated by the dead, who swarm into the sick-rooms of our afflicted humanity, as thick as the frogs of Egypt in the bed-chambers of Pharaoh, there seems to be a grim significance in the use of these words.

To us this outbreak of Satanic empiricism would be a strong presumptive proof that somewhere the Lord is reviving among His people the gifts of Divine healing; and this constant presentation of the devil's coin would lead us to search diligently for the genuine coin bearing Christ's own image and superscription.

A thoughtful writer on this subject has called attention to the fact that the era of modern spiritualism covers almost exactly the era of the alleged revival of the gifts of healing. The most striking instances of professed miraculous cure in modern times happened, as we have shown elsewhere, about fifty years ago in Scotland and in England. The instances have increased and multiplied since, until today the number of devout, prayerful, evangelical Christians who claim to have been miraculously recovered is very large, and their names are sent up from every nation where the Gospel has been preached.

It may be that "the prince of the power of the air, the spirit that now worketh in the children of disobedience," seeing God about to put forth His hand again in signs and wonders, and miracles of healing, has determined, as he is wont, to thwart the Lord by caricaturing His work, and bringing it into contempt in the eyes of His own true people. Thus, perhaps, he has thrown himself into the very path which the Almighty is about to enter, that so he may frighten His Church from treading it.[23]

Or, to state the matter as it seems to us most probable, it may be that the adversary has seized as his most opportune occasion a time when a belief in the supernatural is at its lowest ebb in the Church, and when a denial of modern miracles is well nigh universal among the learned, and that in such a period he is putting forth the most signal displays of superhuman power in order to set his evil impress upon those who may be impressed by these things. Thus he is copying the Lord's own method in using miracles as an evidential testimony, only with this end, to establish "the doctrines of devils;" and to convert people to the creed of the prince of darkness. But are we to turn against the witness of miracles because of this attempt to make it perjure itself in the interest of the evil one? Or, to reverse the hypothesis, and suppose that the evil one is the first to enter this field, then comes the question with equal force, whether because of his preoccupancy we should refuse to go into it, if God's Spirit leads the way. If Antichrist is about to make his mightiest and most malignant demonstration, ought not the Church, if the Lord will give her power, to confront him with sweet and gracious and humble displays of the Spirit's saving health? Here we believe Professor Christlieb speaks again with true scriptural wisdom when he

---

[23] "When men no longer believe in God they begin to believe in ghosts. In truth, there has scarcely ever been an age when men have snatched more greedily after the extravagant than our own which derides the supernatural." Schenkel. Hear also Carlyle's powerful ridicule of Paris casting off God and running after mesmerism: "O women! O men! great is your infidel faith! " "French Revolution," p. 50.

says: "In the last epoch of the consummation of the Church she will again require for the final decisive struggle with the powers of darkness the miraculous interference of her risen Lord; and hence the Scriptures lead us to expect miracles once more for this period." "Modern Doubt and Christian Belief," p. 332. Meanwhile let us be careful that the adversary does not cheat us out of our birthright. If he has set his trademark on miracles, and is using them mightily in his traffic with simple souls; let us not make haste therefore to forfeit whatever right and title in them the Lord has bequeathed to us. Let us not abandon our wheat field because the devil has sowed tares in it. The fact that he sows tares is his testimony to the genuineness of the wheat.

Of course we should expect, in the event of the Church's recovery to any extent of her supernatural gifts, that the enemy would put forth redoubled energy to baffle and confound her. Before a sleeping Church the adversary walks very softly, and modulates his roar to the finest tones, lest he wake her from her slumber. But let her once rise up and take to herself some long disused power, and he will quickly manifest himself in his old character of a "roaring lion walking about seeking whom he may devour."

Erskine, speaking concerning those texts which so clearly confer miraculous gifts upon the Church, says: "I may here remark it, as a striking fact illustrative of the cunning of the prince of darkness, that he has not permitted his instruments to press these texts much, nor to argue from them so triumphantly as they might have done, that the absence of miracles from the Church was a refutation of the Bible. The Bible says, "These signs shall follow them that believe." And yet here is a Church holding this faith and unfollowed by these signs. The ready conclusion from this fact certainly is that the Bible is not true; and we might have expected that this argument would be much used by those who deny the Bible to be a Divine revelation. But it has not been much urged; and why? The subtle enemy of man saw that there was more danger to his own kingdom from the use of this weapon than advantage. It might have led to a result very different from that of disproving the Divine authority of the Bible. There is another conclusion to which it might have led, and that is a lack of faith in the Church. And thus the pressing of this argument might have awakened the Church to a sense of her true condition; and this Satan fears more than the Bible, knowing that a Church asleep is the most powerful weapon against the world— much more powerful than any infidel arguments." "Brazen Serpent," p. 204.

Awake, then, O Church! put on your strength! Awake indeed to evil surmisings and contempt and opprobrium. For none ever yet escaped these things in attempting to revive a forgotten truth. But these may be tokens of the Lord's favor. Certainly they are not the credentials of a slumbering and world-pleasing Church. At all events, let us fear them less than that other alternative—that the heathen shall cry "Where is your God?" and none shall be able to answer "Jehovah Rophi is with us."

# Chapter 8

# THE TESTIMONY OF EXPERIENCE

"Prove me now herewith" is the challenge which the Lord has given in His Word; and there are many in the present generation who have accepted and tested His challenge on the promises of bodily recovery.

We wish in this chapter to consider the experiences and testimony of certain who within our own times have exercised a ministry of healing. Let us not be misunderstood. We do not attribute to any man the power of curing sickness, though we think many are called to be instruments to that end. A physician is a mediator between nature and our suffering humanity; and his skill depends solely upon his ability to interpret and apply the laws of health to the sick, and to bring the sufferer into contact with the recuperative forces of the natural world. In like manner, if the primitive "gifts of healing" are still bestowed in the Church, as we believe, those endowed with them have power only through the mediation of their faith and prayers. We are told that Paul entered into the house of Publius, and, finding his father sick, "prayed and laid his hands on him and healed him." But we do not understand from this that the apostle had any inherent personal power to heal disease; else why did he pray? Prayer is touching the hem of Christ's garment by the human intercessor, while in the laying on of hands he at the same moment touches the body of the sufferer. It is simply, in a word, the repetition of what was done again and again during the earthly ministry of our Lord—the bringing of the sick to Jesus for healing and cleansing. "Why look ye so earnestly on us, as though by our own power or holiness we had made this man to walk?" asks Peter of those who were wondering at the miracle at the Beautiful Gate. If it were a question of human power or holiness we might be quite ready to relegate the gifts of healing to the apostolic age, confessing our utter lack of these qualifications. But since it is a question of the power and holiness of "Jesus Christ, the same yesterday, today, and forever," it is quite another matter. "If thou canst believe" is the question now. "A year famous for believing" is the language in which Romaine designated a certain unusual twelvemonth of his ministry. If such a year should be graciously injected into the calendar of any Christian life it would be a year of success. For believing is knowing God and finding the depths of power and privilege that are hidden for us in Him: and "the people that do know their God shall be strong and do exploits," says the Scripture. Dan. 11:32.

Now, there have been some in our day who have had faith to take the Lord at His word in connection with the promises of healing. And having, as they believed, proved Him, and found Him faithful, their testimony will be deeply instructive to our readers.

Dorothea Trudel is a name especially honored in this relation. The story of her life and labors in connection with the home for invalids in the Swiss village of Mannedorf on Lake Zurich has been very widely read, and has caused great searching of heart in many who have pondered it.[24] The Lord provides deep roots when there are to be wide-spreading branches. And this life, whose boughs so ran over the wall, and stretched beyond the bounds of ordinary service, was unusually rooted and established.

The mother from whom she received her birth and early training was so remarkable for her faith and consecration that, though living in the utmost obscurity and poverty, her biography has been placed among those of the illustrious Christian women of the ages.[25] The wife of a brutal and godless husband, and so cut off from human sympathy that there was none but God to whom she could appeal in her need, she was schooled by this bitter tuition into a life of faith and absolute dependence on God. She looked to Him for food for her family when they must otherwise have starved; for deliverance when they must otherwise have perished; for healing when they must otherwise have died. Dorothea grew up with perpetual exhibitions before her eye of the Lord's restoring of the sick for a poor household which could employ no other physician. The faith which it is so difficult for us to recover was her native inheritance. Hence, what we doubt so painfully whether we may do, she bitterly condemned herself for not doing when she had subsequently neglected it.

After her parents had died we find her engaged in labors of love among the working people; teaching them the Gospel and seeking to lead them to the Savior. How her personal use of the prayer of faith began in connection with these labors she tells in the following words:

"Four of them fell ill, and, as each could do as he pleased, all four summoned a doctor. It was remarked, however, that they got worse after taking the medicine, until, at last, the necessity became so pressing that I went as a worm to the lord, and laid our distress before Him. I told Him how willingly I would send for an elder, as is commanded in James 5, but, as there was not one, I must go to my sick ones in the faith of the Canaanitish woman, and, without trusting to any virtue in my hand, I would lay it upon them. I did so, and, by the lord's blessing, all four recovered. Most powerfully then did the sin of disobeying God's word strike me, and most vividly did the simple life of faith, the carrying out just what God orders, stand before me."

Soon after she gave herself wholly to the Master's work; and as the effects of her evangelistic efforts, and of the answers to her earnest prayers, were noticed, she was importuned to receive patients into her house. Consenting reluctantly, the life-work thus began from which was to flow such a blessing to the souls and bodies of men.

---

[24] "Dorothea Trudel; or, The Prayer of Faith."(London: Morgan and Scott.)
[25] "Consecrated Women." (Hodder and Stoughton.)

Her methods were very simple: the Bible and prayer were her medicines. She dealt with the soul first, using every effort to bring it to faith and obedience to the Gospel; she prayed for the body, laying hands on the sick and anointing them with oil in the name of the Lord. In all this she recognized the necessity of the most absolute consecration on her part and that of her helpers, and of the most surrendering faith on the part of the sick.. Very beautifully does she thus speak of the believer's privilege:

"In the New Testament we are called kings and priests. Power accompanied the anointing of the kings, and if we really belong to the kingly priesthood shall not strength to heal the sick by prayer come on us also through the anointing of the Spirit? If we only wear our Levite dress, and are consecrated in soul and body—if we are only prepared to be vessels of His grace—it is His part to bless. Oh that we were willing not to do more than God would have us do! then would this day be one of great reviving to us."

Thus her work was inaugurated, and thus was she inducted by unseen hands into her remarkable ministry.

Rarely have we traced the story of a life whose consecration was so even and unreserved. Among the sayings which she left on record is this: "The heart ought not to be an inn where the Lord sometimes comes, but a home where He always abides." It was her calling for many years to keep an inn where the sick could lodge, a hospice into which the suffering and distracted wanderer could turn for solace. These came and went with the recurring months, but so constantly was the Lord abiding with her, that it might be said, according to Luther's beautiful simile, that the wayfarer coming and knocking at her heart and asking, "Who lives here?" would hear the instant answer from within, "Jesus Christ." Not that she ever claimed as much, for none was ever more humble and self-depreciatory; but her life declared it. It comes out in her biography that her prayers were sometimes prolonged into midnight: that her soul so wrought with intense desire that often the sweat would stand in beads upon her forehead. Once in busy labors among the sick she passes the whole day without food, utterly forgetting the claims of nature in her absorbing devotion to her work; and then finding it impossible to get food on account of the lateness of the hour, she falls at Jesus' feet, and begs for that meat that the world knows not of, and is so refreshed and filled that she goes all night in the strength of it.

Such rare and Christ-like consecration has always proved an apt soil for the manifestation of the miraculous; especially when chastened and fertilized by bitter persecutions. And this token which the Scripture promises to "all who will live godly in Christ Jesus" was not wanting to her, as the spirit to endure it with unresenting meekness was not wanting. "I have had enemies," she writes, "both known and unknown, in crowds; and thickly scattered falsehoods and slanders were no pleasant portion. I write this with the feeling that whoever cannot bear without emotion even the blackest falsehoods and slanders has yet to experience something of the peace of God, which is like an ocean without bounds."

Medical men and others conceived great hostility to her, and sought to convict her of malpractice in the courts; though it was shown in testimony that most of her patients were such as had spent all their living upon physicians only to be made worse; and that the only medicine she employed was prayer. Speaking of this adversity she says:

"But a storm was now to burst over the work; for in 1856, when the second house was filled with invalids, and the Lord was working mightily, we were fined sixty francs, and were ordered to send away all the patients by a certain time. Though it was the most grievous day of my life, I obeyed the command; but the houses so hastily emptied filled as fast as ever with the blind, the lame, and the deaf, for whom the Lord did great things. Evil spirits were cast out of some of the invalids by prayer, and the sufferer became instantly free. Many were delivered from the power of darkness which had been exercised over their minds, though less visibly and outwardly, and received what we consider the highest and best blessing—that of being changed from wolves into lambs."

In 1861 a second persecution was raised against this most saintly and inoffensive woman. At the instigation of a physician, the magistrates imposed a heavy fine upon her, and ordered her patients to be sent away. Then, through appeal to a higher tribunal, her case was brought into court, and the world was made acquainted, through the testimony of scores of living witnesses, with the wonderful work which God had wrought through her prayers.

Mr. Spondlin, an eminent advocate of Zurich, volunteered to conduct her case; Prelate Von Kopff, Professor Tholuck, and many others, were witnesses on her behalf; and the result was that she was fully acquitted and left undisturbed in her gracious work. Henceforth her house, which had too often through the malice of enemies been a Belhaven, "house of affliction," became only a Bethesda, "house of mercy." If her own simple record, confirmed by the word of scores who bore testimony at her trial, could prove that miracles of healing were wrought in her house, the fact must be considered as established.

With a deep conviction that sin is often the hidden root of sickness, she dealt most earnestly with the souls of her patients. "Confess your faults one to another and pray one for another that ye may be healed," was an injunction that had a deeply practical meaning to her, and often conviction and conversion were the first symptoms of physical convalescence.

"On one occasion a young artisan arrived, in whom cancer had made such progress as to render any approach to him almost unbearable. At the Bible lessons this once frivolous man, now an earnest inquirer, learned where the improvement must begin; and from the day that he confessed his sins against God and man the disease abated. Some time afterwards he acknowledged one sin he had hitherto concealed, and then he speedily recovered his bodily health and returned to his home cured in spirit also."

In some instances her prayers and her eager seeking for the will of God were long continued before any sign of recovery was manifested: in some she gained the strongest impression that it was not the Lord's will to restore them, and then she labored with unceasing diligence to bring them into peace with God before they should die; in others healing was vouchsafed at once.

"A lady in S. had so injured her knee by a fall that for weeks she lay in the greatest agony. The doctor declared that dropsy would supervene, but the heavenly Physician fulfilled those promises which will abide until the end of the world, and by prayer and the laying on of Dorothea's hands the knee was cured in twenty-four hours, and the swelling vanished."

One giving an account of her arraignment says: "During the course of the trial, authenticated cures were brought forward, it is said, to the number of some hundreds. There was one of a stiff knee, that had been treated in vain by the best physicians in France, Germany, and Switzerland; and one of an elderly man who could not walk, and had also been given up by his physicians, but who soon dispensed with his crutches; a man came with a burned foot, and the surgeons said it was a case for 'either amputation or death,' and he also was cured; one of the leading physicians of Wurtemburg testified to the cure of a hopeless patient of his own; another remained six weeks, and says he saw all kinds of sicknesses healed. Cancer and fever have been treated with success; epilepsy and insanity more frequently than any other forms of disease."

Such was the ministry of healing and comfort carried on by this holy woman till the day when she fell asleep in Jesus, and such was the blessed example which she left behind her.

Travellers tell us of a deep and secluded lake in Switzerland in whose crystal mirror the reflection of distant mountains may be seen; though the mountains themselves arc not visible to the eye. In the tranquil, hidden life of this Swiss peasant girl, the image of the invisible Savior was clearly mirrored; , and how many of those who knew her in life, and of those who have read the story of her consecration since her death, have therefrom caught a reflected glimpse of the unseen Redeemer, and been quickened with new love to Him, and a new sense of His present power!

Samuel Zeller took up the work at Mannedorf as it dropped from the dead hands of sister Dorothea. He is the son of the founder of a well-known boys' reformatory at Beuggen, near Basle, and brother-in-law of Gobat, late bishop at Jerusalem. He had been a co-laborer at the home before the death of its founder, and with much prayer that the gifts of faith and of healing might rest upon him she had committed the work to his care. Since her death the institution has continued with no apparent loss of power or usefulness under his direction, he being aided by Miss Zeller, his sister, and by several devoted assistants. All the helpers, even to the servants, render their service as a labor of love, in grateful return in most cases for the recovery which they have received at this home.

Mr. Zeller is a fervent evangelist, going out in every direction preaching the word, as well as laboring "in season, out of season" for the souls and bodies of those who come under his care. From two houses the home has grown to ten, and they are always filled with patients, from many nations. The same methods are employed as under his predecessor. He lays hands upon the sick; he anoints with oil in the name of the Lord, and pleads the promise given in James 5; and his reports published year by year are full of striking instances alike of healing and of conversion.

He entertains no extravagant views of his mission. Holding most tenaciously to the perpetuity of the promise, "The prayer of faith shall save the sick," he yet strongly recognizes the sovereignty of God in the answer. To the question asked by a recent visitor, whether it is not God's will that all His children should be free from sickness, he replied that it is evidently the Father's will that some should overcome sickness and that others should overcome in sickness, and he quoted significantly the words of Hebrews 11:"Some, through faith, subdued kingdoms, wrought righteousness, obtained promises, stopped the mouths of lions, quenched the violence of fire, escaped the edge of the sword, out of weakness were made strong, waxed valiant in fight, turned to flight the armies of the aliens, women received their dead raised to life again. And others were tortured, not accepting deliverance, that they might obtain a better resurrection. And others had trial of cruel mockings and scourgings, yea, moreover, of bonds and imprisonment. They were stoned; they were sawn asunder, were tempted, were slain with the sword; they wandered about in sheepskins and goatskins, being destitute, afflicted, tormented (of whom the world was not worthy); they wandered in deserts, and in mountains, and in dens and caves of the earth. And these all having obtained a good report through faith," etc.

A visit to this home was made a few years since by several eminent German preachers and professors; and when one of these was asked his opinion of the work he answered, "Where the Holy Spirit speaks with so much power, we can do no otherwise than listen to His teaching; critical analysis is out of the question." A quiet and deep spiritual life, a profound faith in the promises of God, and a humble and self-denying surrender to His word and will, are the traits which have characterized the work from the beginning until the present time. The cases of recovery at Mannedorf are so fully given in the report of the Home that we need not here reproduce them.

Pastor Blumhardt, exercising his ministry in the small Lutheran village of Mottlingen, in the heart of the Black Forest, in Germany, is another who was greatly honored of God in his prayers of faith. He died quite recently, but during many years of his active pastorate he was credited with extraordinary grace in praying for the sick. Like others of whom we have spoken, he had the ministry of healing thrust upon him. He first became known for his unusual consecration, and for his zeal and ability in stirring up formal Christians to renewed activity. He prayed for the diseased with such efficacy, and such well-attested cures were reported from his intercessions, that very soon he was resorted to by the suffering from every direction. His home and neighborhood became a hospital, where not only invalids, but sorrowing and sin-sick souls came for counsel and help. One writing of him says, "As regards Blumhardt and his work, it may emphatically be said that the pleasure of the Lord prospered in his hands." He seems to have taken no pains to report his success, having evidently learned the secret that "the way to have a strong faith is to think nothing of yourself." But others praised him, if not his own lips, and he became widely known throughout his country as a pastor who considered the sick bodies of his flock to be under his ministration as well as the sick souls.

We give one instance from the life of Blumhardt, to show the vast influence which a striking exhibition of miraculous power may exert upon the spiritual life of a people.

On commencing his ministry in Mottlingen he found the place fearfully given over to infidelity and sensuality. As his fervent preaching began to tell upon the community, Satan seemed to come in, with great wrath, to resist him. A case occurred in the village which exactly resembled the instances of demoniacal possession recorded in Scripture. The woman thus afflicted endured the most excruciating agony. The pastor being called in was quite appalled, having never seen anything of the kind; and in his perplexity was inclined to be excused from interfering with it. But some of his brethren in the Church, who had listened to his strong utterances on the subject of the prayer of faith, came to him saying, "If you do not wish to shake our belief in your preaching you cannot retreat before the evil one."

After a moment's thought and silent prayer, he answered: "You are right; but to be in accord with the Word of God you must also unite with me in supplication, according to James 5:14." What followed appears from the following account by his friend Pastor Spittler. He says:

"Kindly permit me not to mention in this place the frightful details of her sufferings. The medical man who attended the person was perfectly at a loss as to the case. He said, 'Is there no clergyman in this village who can pray? I can do nothing here.' The minister (Blumhardt) who had then the spiritual care of the village, felt the force of such a reproach, joined as it was to that of his believing people. He went to the house in the strength of faith. The more frightful the manifestations of the destroying power of Satan became, with the more unshaken faith in the all-overcoming power of the living God that pastor continued to struggle against the assaults of the infernal powers, till at last, after a tremendous outcry of the words, 'Jesus is Victor! Jesus is Victor!' heard almost throughout the whole little village, the person found herself freed from all the dreadful chains under which she had sighed so long, and often come to the very brink of death.

"That voice, 'Jesus is Victor!' sounded like a trumpet of God through the village. After a week one man of very loose and deceitful character, whom the pastor on that account felt almost afraid of approaching, came trembling and pale to Blumhardt into his study, and said, 'Sir, is it then possible that I can be pardoned and saved? I have not slept for a whole week, and if my heart be not eased it will kill me.' He made an astonishing confession of iniquity, which for the first time opened the pastor's eyes to the multitude and enormity of sins prevailing among the people. The pastor prayed with him, and put Christ before him in His readiness to pardon even the vilest of sinners that would come to Him for mercy. When the man seemed completely cast down and almost in despair, Blumhardt found it his duty, as an ambassador of Christ, solemnly to assure him of God's mercy in Jesus Christ; and lo! immediately his countenance was changed, beaming with joy and gratitude.

"The first thing which the man now did was to go to his fellow-sinners, from cottage to cottage, and tell them what he had just experienced. First they were astonished, and could not understand it; yet they saw the marvellous change in him. He urged them to go to the minister about their souls; some he even dragged as it were in triumph to the manse, till about twenty persons were in the same way convinced of sin, and found grace and forgiveness in Jesus."[26]

Then follows the account of a most gracious and widespread revival. The whole village became a Bochim. With tears and lamentations the people came confessing their sins, and inquiring the way of escape from the wrath of God that was resting upon them. The pastor's house was besieged from morning to night with penitents, so that within two months, as he declared, there were not twenty persons in the place who had not come to him bewailing their sins and finding peace in Jesus Christ. The transformation which resulted was hardly less wonderful than that which occurred in Kidderminster under the preaching of Richard Baxter. The story gives a most striking indication of what might result even now, under the preaching of the Gospel "with signs following."

"The soul is the life of the body; faith is the life of the soul; Christ is the life of faith"—so wrote the good John Flavel; and thus he traced very obviously and directly the course through which Christ the Redeemer acts upon the human body.

Pastor Otto Stockmayer might be fitly named the theologian of the doctrine of healing by faith. He has given some very subtle, not to say bold and startling expositions of the relation of sin and sickness, "The soul is the life of the body," and the Lord does not intend that His saving and sanctifying ministry shall stop with the regeneration and renewal of the soul, is Stockmayer's strongly-asserted doctrine.

Attaching great weight to the words of Scripture which declare that Christ "healed all that were sick, that it might be fulfilled which was spoken by Esaias the prophet, saying, Himself took our infirmities and bare our sicknesses," he reasons that if our Redeemer bore our sicknesses it is not His will that His children should remain under the power of disease, any more than that having borne our sins it is His will that they should remain under condemnation and disobedience. He says:

---

[26] "Pastor Blumhardt and His Work" (London: Morgan and Scott).

"Once understanding that it is not the will of God that His children should be sick (James 5:14-18), and that Christ has redeemed us from our sickness as from our sins (Matt. 8:16, 17), we can no longer look upon healing as a right which it would be lawful for us to renounce. It is no longer a question whether we wish to be healed: God's will must be fulfilled in our bodies as well as in our souls. Our beloved Lord must not be robbed of a part of the heritage of His agony.

"It is by virtue of a Divine will that the offering of the body of Jesus Christ has sanctified us (Heb. 10:10), which means that Christ by His death has withdrawn the members of our body, with our entire being, from every sacrilegious end or use. He has regained and consecrated them for His own exclusive and direct use.

"Wrested by Christ's ransom from all foreign power, from the power of sin or of sickness or of the devil, our members must remain intact, surrendered to Him who has redeemed them.

"Let my people go," was God's word to Pharaoh;and such is God's command to sin and sickness, and to Satan: 'Let my people go that they may serve me.'

"Thus God's children must not seek the healing of the body without taking at the same time, by faith, all the new position which Christ's redemption gives us—and which is expressed in these words of Moses to Pharaoh; or better still in Paul's words (2 Cor. 5:14, 15), which amount to this—Nothing more for self, but all for Christ. Before seeking freedom from sickness we must lay hold of the moral freedom which the Redemption of Christ has obtained for us, and by which we are cut off from any self-seeking: from the seeking of our own will, our own life, our own interests, or our own glory. Our members are henceforth Christ's, and neither for ourselves nor for our members, but for Christ and for His members, we desire health. We knew none other but Christ." This in brief is the doctrine of Pastor Stockmayer as set forth in a tract entitled "Sickness and the Gospel," (Partridge and Co.) which has passed through many editions and been very widely read. As the minister of a Christian flock his practice has conformed to his teaching. He has used the same methods as those employed at Mannedorf; and he has now a home in Hauptwiel, Thurgau, Switzerland, for the reception of such as desire to be healed through prayer.

Pastor Rein is another of the same group of primitive teachers and ministers. He was greatly esteemed while living, and it is only a few years since he fell asleep. He began his service in the Gospel as a decided formalist. But shutting himself up to the Bible and determining to shape his ministry rigidly by its teachings, without regard to tradition, a great change came over him. He now abandoned the habit of reading prayers at the bedside of the sick, and began to pour out petitions directly from the heart. Later he felt constrained to use the practice of laying hands on them while praying, according to the word of the Lord in Mark 16. Still later he began to anoint with oil in the name of the Lord in connection with his praying for the sick—carrying out strictly the directions given in the Epistle of James. His ministry seems to have been as conspicuous for its humility as for its zeal and consecration; and diligent care for the welfare of others so marked his course, that he may be said to have illustrated the maxim that "true humility consists not so much in thinking meanly of ourselves as in not thinking of ourselves at all."

From a very tender tribute to his life which recently appeared we make the following extract:[27]

"When sick people were brought to him he received them as sent by the Lord. Much blessing and consolation was found in the silence and retirement of the simple cure of Pastor Rein. He loved to work for the kingdom of God in self-renunciation and always in silence, without show, and he always shrank from being spoken of. Oh, how blessed it is when the word of God accompanied with prayer is used as the medicine of the body as well as soul!

"Rein never employed a doctor, believing in the words of Exodus 15:26—'I am the Lord that healeth thee,' or, as it is in many translations, 'I am the Lord thy physician.' When he was ill the elders of his Church or his friends laid hands on him and prayed over him, and he was always better than if he had taken medicine; he was kept in a greater calm, and his communion with God was not interrupted by the doctor's visits, and by the continual occupation of punctually following their directions. He lived in such intimate relation with God that he asked Him for all he wanted, the greatest and the least things alike. This was why he could not except even healing, and he shrank from seeking any help but that which came directly from God.

"He was jealous for God that He alone should have the glory. That which grieved him deeply was to see how little glory is given to God in general, and especially in the cure of illness, which is attributed generally to doctors or to medicine. Thus he would not allow any remedy to come between him and his God, and he rejoiced with all his heart when he saw others leave the old track of this world's law of prudence, to follow the path of an obedient and unreserved faith.

"When he prayed over and laid hands on the sick he watched attentively for a knowledge of God's will regarding the person whom he was occupied with, and always besought Him to reveal to him whether the sickness was unto death, or whether it was rather a merciful visitation, sent to lead the subject of it to reflection; and he prayed accordingly.

"This confidence in God, which made him renounce all human means in illness, caused him to be much criticised. But we must say, to his honor, that Rein was extremely charitable towards others, never seeking to put a yoke upon them or to lay down the law to them, in that which he looked upon as a permission, a precious grace from on high.

"He never regarded it as a sin in any one to take medicine, or to consult a doctor, when they had not the special faith to do without them—a faith which, very precious as it is, is not necessary for salvation. Who can find fault with such

---

[27] See "Israel's Watchman," Aug., 1878.

as declare, like Rein, that they cannot do otherwise than commit themselves solely to God in all things, even for bodily health, and that they esteem as happy those who can do the same?

"He was actuated by a holy jealousy, when he heard the signs which should follow them that believe (Mark 16:17, 18) spoken of as belonging only to apostolic times, instead of its being recognized that it is owing to the decline of faith that these signs no longer exist. It has been said that Faith is God's power placed at man's disposition. So he believed, and on this principle he acted."

Several interesting incidents of recovery under his prayers are given in connection with this sketch of his life, but they are of the same type as those elsewhere recorded, and we will not reproduce them.

Among other evangelists and pastors who hold the same faith and practice as these we may mention Lord Radstock. A very devoted and deeply spiritual man he is known to be by all who have come in contact with him , and many who have never seen him have read with interest of his evangelistic work among the higher ranks, especially in Russia. and Sweden. Writing to "The Christian" concerning his work in the latter country, he sends reports of several very striking instances of cure in answer to prayer, and says:

"One interesting feature of the Lord's grace in Stockholm is the obedience of faith with which several pastors and elder brethren have accepted their privilege of anointing the sick and praying over them in the name of the Lord. There have been many remarkable instances of God's gracious healing. I enclose details of a few cases, that God's children may be encouraged to see that God has not withdrawn the promise in James 5:15, and that it is better to trust in the Lord than to put confidence in man.

In America there are several homes for healing conducted on the same principle as that of Miss Trudel. Quite a number of them are under the direction of pious women, who have learned the secret of the prayer of faith. We have only space to refer to one work which is most widely known through its published reports, and of which, from his near neighborhood to it, the writer has had an excellent opportunity to judge.

Dr. Charles Cullis is at the head of what is known as the "Faith-work" in the city of Boston. The work has many branches: the Consumptives' Home; the Willard Tract Repository; homes for children; city mission work; foreign missionary work; schools among the freedmen, etc., all maintained upon the same principle virtually as the orphan work of George Muller, at Bristol. And one who has been made acquainted with a single department of this enterprise— as, for example, that of the Consumptives' Home—can have no doubt as to the most beneficent and Christ-like character of the labors there carried on.

Dr. Cullis has for several years been accustomed, when applied to, to minister to the sick in the manner above described. And there are among us many unimpeachable witnesses to the answers which have been granted for the recovery from disease. The writer is well acquainted with quite a number of these—some of several years' standing—and has no hesitation in saying that they bear every evidence of genuineness. How Dr. Cullis was led to exercise this ministry is best told in his own words, which we extract from his published report called "Faith Cures."

"For several years my mind had been exercised before God as to whether it was not His will that the work of faith in which He had placed me should extend to the cure of disease as well as the alleviation of the miseries of the afflicted. I often read the instructions and promise contained in the fourteenth and fifteenth verses of the fifth chapter of the Epistle of James.

"They seemed so very plain that I often asked of my own heart, Why, if I can rely on God's word, 'Whatsoever ye shall ask in my name, that will I do,' and every day verify its truth in the supply of the daily needs of the various work committed to my care,—why cannot I also trust Him to fulfil His promises as to the healing of the body, 'The prayer of faith shall save the sick, and the Lord shall raise him up'? I could not see why, with such explicit and unmistakable promises, I should limit the present exercise of God's power. I began to inquire of earnest Christians whether they knew of any instances of answer to prayer for the healing of the body. Soon afterwards the Life of Dorothea Trudel fell into my hands, which strengthened my convictions, and raised the inquiry, 'If God can perform such wonders in Mannedorf, why not in Boston?'

"At this time I had under my professional care a Christian lady, with a tumor which confined her almost continuously to her bed in severe suffering. All remedies were unavailing, and the only human hope was the knife; but feeling in my heart the power of the promise, I one morning sat down by her bedside, and taking up the Bible, I read aloud God's promise to His believing children: 'And the prayer of faith shall save the sick, and the Lord shall raise him up; and if he have committed sins, they shall be forgiven him.'

"I then asked her if she would trust the Lord to remove this tumor and restore her to health and to her missionary work. She replied, 'I have no particular faith about it, but am willing to trust the Lord for it.'

"I then knelt and anointed her with oil in the name of the Lord, asking Him to fulfil His own word. Soon after I left, she got up and walked three miles. From that time the tumor rapidly lessened, until all trace of it at length disappeared."

The work thus begun has gone on now for quite a number of years, and we think there can be no reasonable doubt that in Boston, as well as in Mannedorf and in Mottlingen, there has been a living and repeated demonstration that God is still pleased to recover the sick directly and manifestly in answer to His people's intercessions.

If these things be so, can any say that we have not reason to praise God and rejoice with new joy in Him

"Who forgiveth all thine iniquities
Who healeth all thy diseases"?

"Any explanation but the admission of the miraculous," is the cry which an unbelieving world raises when anything wonderful happens. And Christians more solicitous for their caution than for their faith have sometimes joined in the cry. And thus the seal of the supernatural has been assiduously withheld, we fear, where it should have been permitted to place its impress and testimony. But we do not so much call attention to these instances of healing as to these examples of faith. There may be mistakes in the estimates put upon the cures, but can there be any in the sure word of promise? If any of these testimonies of recovery should prove ill-founded, it would only demonstrate the ignorance of men. But God has in the last days spoken to us by His Son, and "he that receiveth His testimony hath set to his seal that God is true."

# Chapter 9
# THE TESTIMONY OF THE HEALED

"One thing I know, that whereas I was blind I now see." This confession of experience has always been regarded as the strongest that can be made. The "I know" indeed may seem to savor of egotism and assurance. But let us not forget that while the egotism of opinion is always offensive, the egotism of experience can never be rebuked. Is it the highest attainment of mere human thought and speculation to know that one does not know? Hence very fittingly we have the culture of our age graduating in agnosticism, which is knowledge culminating in ignorance, as the highest mountain peaks are lost in the clouds. On the other hand, when we read the opening words of John's first epistle—"that which we have heard, which we have seen with our eyes, which we have looked upon, and our hands have handled of the word of life"—we are not surprised at the writer's constant use of the words "we know," or that he is able to say, "Hereby we do know that we know Him."

Experience is the surest touchstone of truth. It is not always infallible indeed, especially when it deals with our spiritual states and conditions. For these are often deceptive and difficult to interpret. But certainly one ought to know when an infirmity which has long oppressed the body has been removed, or when a pain that has incessantly tortured the nerves has ceased. This is a kind of testimony which is not easily ruled out of court.

And there are many who stand ready to give in this witness. Ought we to refuse to hear it, or to dismiss it as visionary and idle talk? We are quite accustomed to accept what we call a religious experience as a test of fitness for church membership. Is it less difficult to recognize and interpret a physical experience?

Let us listen to the statements of some who have told the story of their bodily healing. We cite as our first example that of Miss Fancourt, of London, the daughter of an English clergyman, whose case created no small interest at the time of its publication.

The story of her sickness is too long to be given in detail. Suffice it to say that she was attacked with severe hip disease in November 1822. From this date till 1828 she was a constant sufferer, not only from the disease itself, but from the varied operations of leeches, blisters, bleedings, and cuttings of the surgeon's knife, and all to no effect. From this period onward for two years she was a helpless cripple, for most of the time confined to her bed. The story of her recovery we give in her own words:

"Thus it continued till the 20th of October, 1830, when a kind friend who had seen me about two months before had been led by God to pray earnestly for my recovery, remembering what is written, "Whatsoever ye shall ask in prayer, believing, ye shall receive." He asked in faith, and God graciously answered his prayer. On Wednesday night, my friend being about to leave the room, Mr. J. begged to be excused a short time. Sitting near me, we talked of his relations and of the death of his brother; rising, he said, 'They will expect me at supper,' and put out his hand. After asking some questions respecting the disease, he added, 'It is melancholy to see a person so constantly confined.' I answered, 'It is sent in mercy.' 'Do you think so? Do you not think the same mercy could restore you?' God gave me faith, and I answered, 'Yes.' 'Do you believe Jesus could heal as in old times?' 'Yes.' 'Do you believe it is only unbelief that prevents it?' 'Yes.' 'Do you believe that Jesus could heal you at this very time?' 'Yes.' Between these questions he was evidently engaged in prayer. 'Then,' he added, 'rise up and walk; come down to your family.' He then had hold of my hand; he prayed to God to glorify the name of Jesus. I rose from my couch quite strong. God took away all my pains, and we walked down stairs, Mr. J. praying most fervently, 'Lord have mercy upon us; Christ have mercy upon us.' Having been down a short time, finding my handkerchief left on the couch, taking the candle I fetched it. The next day I walked more than a quarter of a mile; and on Sunday from the Episcopalian chapel, distance of one mile and a quarter. Up to this time God continues to strengthen me, and I am perfectly well. To Jesus be all the glory. November 13, 1830." Mrs. Oliphant's "Life of Edward Irving."

We have the added information that this longsuffering invalid continued to be well, and that the story of her healing, so soon as it went abroad, drew down upon her and her family a most violent storm of ridicule and obloquy. By the religious press which took up the matter the story was treated as a gross scandal upon the Christian faith; and so bitter were the reflections upon the parties involved that the venerable father of the lady, though hitherto a confessed disbeliever in modern miracles, felt called upon to publish his emphatic confirmation of the story. The following is the statement of the Rev. Mr. Fancourt:

"Under this peculiar dispensation of mercy there rests on my mind a solemn conviction that the glory of God and the interest of religion are deeply involved in the publicity which it will probably acquire. But without shrinking from the responsibility attached to the declaration, I profess myself ready to bear my open testimony to a notable fact: namely, that as I view it God has raised an impotent cripple, in the person of my youngest daughter, to instantaneous soundness of her bodily limbs by faith in the name of Jesus, being taught by her mother Church to know and feel that there is none other name under heaven given to man in whom and through whom she could receive health and salvation, but only the name of our Lord Jesus Christ. In this faith, through the instrumentality of the effectual fervent prayer of a righteous man (for God heareth not sinners), which availeth much, God has done exceeding abundantly above all that we could ask or think. I am aware that there are questions of difficult solution as to the instrumentality by which the benefit has been bestowed; but who would not tremble at the fearful conclusion which would result from a denial of the Divine interposition? Deprecating such a thought, I feel persuaded that they are most on the side of truth and soberness who unite with us in telling the Church that God hath done great things for us, whereof we are glad, which in their first communication made us like them that dream."

We cannot help pausing upon the lesson suggested by this incident. Strange, it might be said, that the sufferer should be grudged her release from pain and helplessness. If a supernatural cure could not be admitted, it would seem that at least none would envy her the harmless illusion. Yet has it not been so from the beginning? "We must admit any solution rather than a miracle," said the Christian Observer, commenting on this cure. And we remember that the wise Jews said about the healing of another cripple, "that indeed a notable miracle has been done by them is manifest to all them that dwell in Jerusalem, and we cannot deny it," as if to say, "we have done our best to disprove it." Evidently our Lord anticipated this treatment of miracles of healing when He introduced them; for He said, "Go and show John again those things which ye do hear and see: the blind receive their sight, and the lame walk, the lepers are cleansed, and the deaf hear, the dead are raised up, and the poor have the Gospel preached to them. And "blessed is he whosoever shall not be offended in me." The last thing, it would seem, at which the world should take offence. That the prison doors should be opened, and light and sound be let in upon poor immured and darkened souls; that lame feet wearily dragged by bodies which they were made to bear up should be rendered whole and elastic by the Healer's touch; that lepers should be released from their ghastly malady, and the dead be given back to their friends,—are these events that should give offence? Alas at what antipodes man's anger often stands to Christ's. The rulers of the synagogue "answered with indignation" because on the Sabbath day the Lord had healed a suffering woman whom Satan had bound for eighteen years. Once we hear of the mighty indignation of Christ. At the tomb of Lazarus Jesus was "indignant in spirit," for so they tell us the words mean. He saw the masterpiece of the devil, whose works He had come to destroy, spread out before Him—death, and the tears, the anguish, and the groans that follow in death's train; and His soul was stirred to holy wrath within Him. Do we well to be angry at the suggestion that even now the Lord of life may snatch from sickness, death's forerunner, those upon whom He has laid His hand?

We give the following instance which we find recorded and strongly endorsed by an eminent Baptist minister of the last century, Rev. Morgan Edwards, of New Jersey. We reproduce the story of the "miracle," as he names it, in his own somewhat quaint and old-fashioned phraseology. It is in regard to Hannah Carman, who, he says, died in Brunswick, N. J., 1776. He says:

"Of her I received the following piece of history, so well attested that the sceptic himself can have nothing to gainsay. I have before me three certificates of the fact, and the testimony of Squire N. Stout's lady, who was present at the time of the miracle. She was remarkable for piety and good sense from a child. About the twenty-fifth year of her age she got a fall from a horse, which so hurt her back that she was bowed down and could in nowise lift up herself. Her limbs were also so affected that she was a perfect cripple, not able to walk nor to help herself in the smallest matters. One day the young woman who had the care of her (now Squire Stout's lady), seated her in an elbow chair, and went to the garden. She had not been long in the garden before she heard a rumbling noise in the house. She hastened in, thinking that the cripple had tumbled out of her chair; but how was she surprised and frightened to see the cripple in the far end of the room praising God, who had made her whole every whit! Miss Ketcham (for that was the name of Squire N. Stout's lady, from whom I had the narrative) sent to her neighbor Bray (the signer of one of my certificates), who came in haste, and was equally astonished, for the cripple was all the while in an ecstasy, taking no notice of the company, but running about the house, moving chairs and tables from place to place, going to her bedroom, taking up her bed and walking about with it, and every now and then falling on her knees to praise God, who had made whole a daughter of Abraham, who had been bowed down for ten or a dozen years. It has been observed before that the cripple was alone in the house when the miraculous event occurred. The manner thereof must have come from herself, and was as follows: "While I was musing on these words, "Eneas, Jesus Christ maketh thee whole," I could not help breathing out my heart and my soul in the following manner: "O that I had been in Eneas's place!" Upon that I heard an audible voice saying, "Arise, take up thy bed and walk!" The suddenness of the voice made me start in my chair; but how was I astonished to find my back strengthening and my limbs recovering their former use in that start! I got up, and to convince myself that it was a reality and not a vision, I lifted up my chair and whatever came in my way; went to my room and took up my bed, and put my strength to other trials, till I was convinced that the cure was real, and not a dream or delusion."" "Materials for History of the Baptists in New Jersey," 1792, p. 63.

Edwards adds: "I doubt not but some witlings will find pleasantry in this story. Let them; and be their pleasantry their reward. But whoever believes in the power of ejaculatory prayer will be benefitted by it."

The witlings, it would seem, then made sport of this story of healing, as of the one just before referred to. But, considering the eminent character of the man who vouches for it, and the certificates to the truth of the narrative of which he speaks, is there not a fair presumption at least in favor of its genuineness? We shall be regarded as very simple, no doubt, for having reproduced the tale; but no matter; simplicity is one of the soft and formative stages of all true faith. The first announcements of the resurrection were deemed as "idle tales" by those who heard them; and had it not been for the credulity of the simple-minded women who first reported this miracle, we might not soon have had the faith of the strong-minded men, who afterwards preached it. Professor Godet, alluding to alleged miracles among the French Protestants, which have precisely the same kind of documentary evidence in their favor, strongly refuses to pronounce against them, and quotes with approval the following weighty words: "There was a time when men believed everything; in our day they believe nothing. I think we should take a middle course; we should not believe everything, but we ought to believe some things. For this spirit of incredulity and strong-mindedness answers no good purpose, and I have not discovered its use. Is it possible that God has so hidden Himself behind the creatures of His hand and under the veil of secondary causes that He will never lift the curtain at all? Let us conclude that the credulity of our ancestors caused many fictions to be received as good history, but also that incredulity causes good history to pass in our day for worthless stories." "Defense of the Christian Faith," p. 88.

The following narrative of a well-known physician, Dr. R— of Philadelphia, is certainly very striking. It is given in his own words as published in "The Great Physician," by Dr. Boardman. Being asked to give an account of the recovery of his son, Dr. R— said:

"I do not like to speak of it to people generally, they are so unbelieving; but I can tell you. The children were jumping off from a bench, and my little son fell and broke both bones of his arm below the elbow. My brother, who is a professor of surgery in the College at Chicago, was here on a visit. I asked him to set and dress the arm. He did so; put it in splints, bandages, and in a sling. The child was very patient, and went about without a murmur all that day. The next morning he came to me and said, 'Dear papa, please take off these things.' 'Oh no, my son: you will have to wear these things five or six weeks before it will be well.' 'Why, papa, it is well.' 'Oh no, my dear child, that is impossible.' 'Why, papa, you believe in prayer, don't you?' 'You know I do, my son.' 'Well, last night when I went to bed it hurt me very bad, and I asked Jesus to make it well, and He did make it well, and it is well.'

"I did not like to say a word to chill his faith. A happy thought came: I said, 'My dear child, your uncle put the things on, and if they are taken off he must do it.' Away he went to his uncle, who told him he would have to go as he was six or seven weeks, and must be very patient; and when the little fellow told him that Jesus had made him well, he said, 'Pooh! pooh! nonsense,' and sent him away. The next morning the poor boy came again to me, and pleaded with so much sincerity and confidence that I more than half believed that he was really healed, and went to my brother and said, 'Had you not better undo his arm and let him see for himself?—then he will be satisfied. If you do not, I fear, though he is very obedient, he may be tempted to undo it himself, and then it may be worse for him.' My brother yielded, took off the bandages and splints, and exclaimed, 'It is well—absolutely well,' and hastened to the door for air, to keep from fainting.

"He had been a real, simple-hearted Christian, but in his student days wandered away; but this brought him back to the Lord. Strange if it had not! To all this I could say nothing, if I had been ever so much disposed, in the way of accounting for it, upon any other hypothesis than that of the little fellow himself—that Jesus had made him well."

A marvelous story, you will exclaim; but is it not especially wonderful that we find the doctors of medicine as the witnesses to a miracle? They who handle human wounds with the callous fingers of science, cry out, "Lo, God was in this place!" while we theologians are such devotees to cause and effect that we fear we may commit sacrilege by bringing in the Cause of causes. But it may be that the physicians and physiologists are bolder than we in personalizing the mysterious agency which operates in the cure of the sick. They call it the "vis medicatrix," as if it were "some gentle feminine nurse hidden from the sight, whose office it is to expel the poisons, knit the fractures, and heal the bodies." Would that we were quite as bold to recognize sometimes, at least, the Holy Spirit as our Healer, and to pay that only fee which He requires—our open acknowledgment and thanks to Him who has said, "I am the Lord that healeth thee." And we must express our decided conviction that, on the whole, Christian physicians are less sceptical on the question of miraculous healing than Christian ministers; at least, we know more of them in our day who have orally or in writing given in their adherence to this doctrine than of preachers and theologians. In the narrative next following we have the beautiful sight of the beloved physician spending the night in prayer with a few friends who have come to ask the recovery of his long-suffering patient. In Dr. Boardman's book we read the tender story of an English physician, Dr. de Gorrequer Griffeth, leaving a little patient for whom his skill could avail nothing, and going down by the river side, whither he had been wont to resort, for communion with God, and there asking and receiving the recovery of the child. The two persons who have been most largely used in praying for the cure of the sick in our own city are educated and practicing physicians. We to whom are committed the oracles of God do well to see to it that we are not more sceptical than they to whom are entrusted the pharmacopoeia of nature.

We instance another cure, the story of which has been read by many, and heard by not a few from the lips of the emancipated sufferer herself. The remarkable history of Miss Jennie Smith, of Philadelphia, is rehearsed in the little book, "From Baca to Beulah." Garrigues Bros., Philadelphia, 1880.

Her disease, so mysterious and agonizing and long-continued that her pastor pronounced it "a narrative of suffering rarely if ever equalled," cannot be described at length here. Suffice it to say that she was a helpless cripple for about sixteen years, suffering much of the time the extremest agony. One limb was subject to such violent and uncontrollable spasms that it had to be confined in a strong box, and often held down by heavy weights. During her extraordinary sufferings her faith and consecration seem to have been brought into very lively exercise; so that making her couch a pulpit, she was greatly used for quickening the spiritual life of such as came within her reach. Meantime she began to lay hold of the promise of God for bodily healing, and getting tokens of His power in several partial reliefs, she was led on to ask and obtain entire recovery. The story of this we give in her own words. After a day of unusual suffering a few Christian friends had gathered about her in the evening as she lay in her extension chair. She says:

"The evening was devoted to prayer, led by Pastor Everett. After the first hour or more, some were obliged to leave. One brother, whom I had not met before, as he shook hands on leaving, said, 'My sister, you are asking too much; you are too anxious to get well. The Lord can make better use of you upon your cot than upon your feet.' I was thankful for the brother's words. I then looked searchingly into my heart. The blessed Lord knows I honestly answered, 'No, I am not anxious to get well; I have gained the victory over that. If the heat of the furnace were increased a thousandfold I could say, Thy will be done, and feel pain would be sweet if fully shown to me that it is the Father's will that I should suffer. And I believe the time has come for me to know that will.'

"Up to this point of the meeting there was not that oneness of mind that I felt there must be. I said to those who remained, 'Can you tarry with me till the morning if need be? I feel that it must be by waiting that our Father will give us the blessing. Are we of one accord in this matter?' My physician, Dr. Morgan, was the first to say, 'I will stay, and I fully agree with you.'

"They all gathered about my chair. Never can that little group forget that season. It was now after nine o'clock. We continued waiting before the Lord. Occasionally one or another would quote, with comment, an appropriate text of Scripture, or engage in a brief prayer. For myself, I lay in quiet expectancy, still suffering, but with a remarkable sense of the Divine presence. Much of the time I was almost oblivious to my surroundings, so engaged was I in communion with my heavenly Father. About eleven o'clock I was led to vocally offer myself to God in fresh consecration, saying: 'I give this body anew—these eyes to see, these lips to talk, these ears to hear, and, if it be Thy will, these feet to walk for Jesus. All that is of me—all, all is Thine, dear Father. Only let Thy precious will be done.'

"Up to this time there was no cessation from suffering or increase of strength. As before said, I was weaker than usual. After a brief silence there suddenly flashed upon me a most vivid view of the healing of the withered arm. It seemed to me I could see it being thrust out whole. At the same instant the Holy Spirit bestowed on my soul a faith to claim a similar blessing. It seemed as if heaven were at that moment opened, and I was conscious of a baptism of strength, as sensibly and as positively as if an electric shock had passed through my system. I felt definitely the strength come into my back, and into my helpless limbs. Laying my hand on the chair-arms, I raised myself to a sitting posture. The Garrigues brothers, being seated on either side of the chair, naturally sprang forward and laid hold to assist me. This, however, was not necessary. Dr. Morgan, who was sitting near, stepped forward and let down the foot-board, and while the hands of my friends were yet on my shoulders I arose and stood upon my feet.

"Sister Fannie could not remember ever having seen me standing up. She was so startled she threw up both hands and screamed, 'Oh, Jennie, Jennie!' No words can express my feelings. My very being yet thrills with praise as I speak of that hour. As I stood Brother W. H. G— placed his hand upon my head, saying, 'Praise God from whom all blessings flow.'

"My first thought was 'Can I kneel?' I asked to do so, and knelt as naturally as if I had been accustomed to it. There was so much of the Divine presence that not a word was spoken. We poured forth our souls in silent thanksgiving and praise. I then arose and walked across the room with entire ease and naturalness; there were no pricking or otherwise unpleasant sensations. Sat down in a rocking-chair for some minutes. It seemed so wonderful that I did not have to learn to walk. My limbs and body seemed as if made new."

A case so widely known as this has been could not fail to elicit considerable comment. How was such a rapid and complete recovery effected? Some said that it was doubtless owing to a sudden and powerful reassertion of the will; that, as in many such obscure diseases, the ill was probably nervous and largely imaginary, and their prayers and faith simply brought courage and reassurance. Indeed!—and is it not a great thing even to find a physician who can discover that nothing ails us when all the doctors have pronounced it a desperate case? If this were all—which we do not for a moment admit—it would certainly be a vast triumph of faith-healing over medication. For it is not alone that our poor diseased humanity needs a physician with Divine skill to remove our deep-seated sicknesses, but especially one with Divine insight to fathom and uncover them. The doctor's eyes are often more at fault than his hand. He cannot cure because he cannot comprehend the secret of our plague. How wonderful is the insight of the Great Physician! His penetrating glance goes to the root of disease when ours can only see the symptoms.

Never was there healer with such vision as His.

"He took our suffering human race,
He read each wound and weakness clear,
He struck his finger on the place,
And said, Thou ailest here and here."

Blessed is the patient who has found a Doctor whose healing touch is guided ever by that clear and unerring sight which knows what is in man, and needs not that any should testify of Him.

Of this instance we have the doctor's written statement, confirming in every particular the testimony of his patient, both as to the fearful character of her sickness and her sudden and complete recovery in answer to prayer. We might bring forward many more witnesses did space permit. The instances of drunkards cured at once of long enthralling appetite; of the victims of opium saved from their degrading bondage, and all traces of the habit taken away, are especially interesting as evidences of God's immediate action in taking away the consequences of sin, as well as forgiving the sin itself.

If one's eye is open, and his mind unprejudiced, how many of such traces of God's finger will he see in the world—events clear and unmistakable enough for him who is willing to believe, but questionable and uncertain enough for him who is determined to deny.

# Chapter 10

# THE VERDICT OF CANDOR

In summing up what has been brought forward in the preceding chapters, we wish to review briefly the theory, the testimony, and the practice, which our discussion has involved.

As to the theory: Is it right for us to pray to God to perform a miracle of healing in our behalf? "The truth is," answers an eminent writer, "that to ask God to act at all, and to ask Him to perform a miracle, are one and the same thing." Jellett, "Efficacy of Prayer," p. 41. That is to say, a miracle is the immediate action of God, as distinguished from His mediate action through natural laws. We see no reason, therefore, why we should hesitate to pray for the healing of our bodies any more than for the renewal of our souls. Both are miracles; but both are covered and provided for by the same clear word of promise.

Our hesitancy to ask for physical healing we believe to rest largely on a false and widespread error in regard to the relation of the human body to the redemption of Christ. It is taken for granted by many that this house of clay was never intended either to be repaired or beautified by the renewing Spirit. The caged-eagle theory of man's existence is widely prevalent—the notion that the soul is imprisoned in flesh, and is beating its bars in eager longing to fly away and be at rest—all of which may be very good poetry, but is very bad divinity. The Scripture teaches indeed that "we that are in this tabernacle do groan being burdened;" but it does not therefore thrust death's writ of ejection into our hands as our great consolation, and tell us that our highest felicity consists in moving out of this house as quickly as possible. "Not for that we would be unclothed, but clothed upon, that mortality might be swallowed up of life," is the inspired testimony concerning our highest hope of existence. The redemption of the body, not its dissolution—resurrection, not death, is set before us in the Gospel as the true goal of victory. But because that great promise of the Gospel, "Who shall fashion anew the body of our humiliation that it may be conformed to the body of His glory," has been so largely supplanted by the notion of a spiritual elimination taking place at death, in which a purified soul is forever freed from an encumbering body,—all this has been changed in the creed of many. The heresy of death-worship has supplanted the doctrine of resurrection, with a multitude of Christians, because they have allowed the partial felicity, the departing to be with Christ, to take the place of the final victory, the coming of Christ, to quicken our mortal bodies by His Spirit that dwells in us.

It is easy to see now that when death gets established in the high esteem of Christians, sickness, his prime minister, should come to be held in great regard also. And so it is, that while very few enjoy being sick, very many are afraid seriously to claim healing, lest it should seem like rebellion against a sacred ordinance, or a revolt from a hallowed medicine which God is mercifully putting to their lips for their spiritual recovery. Those who have such a feeling should search the Scriptures to learn how constantly sickness is referred to as the work of the devil. From the day when "Satan went forth from the presence of the Lord and smote Job with sore boils," to the hour when the deliverer came and loosed "a daughter of Abraham, whom Satan had bound, lo, these eighteen years,"—he that "hath the power of death, that is the devil," has been compelling our wretched race to reap the firstfruits of mortality, disease and pain and bodily decay. Alas if the Lord's people shall be so deceived by him that they shall willingly accept sickness, the firstfruits of death, as their portion, instead of seeking for health, the firstfruits of redemption! If any shall insist, indeed, that God often allows His servants to be sick for their good, or that He sometimes permits them to fall into sin for their chastening, on that account we shall not admit that sickness is God's agent, any more than that sin is. An old divine probably spoke as truly as he did quaintly when he said that "the Lord sometimes allows His saints to be sharpened on the devil's grindstone," but we believe that in the comprehensive petition, "Deliver us from the evil one," is contained without question a prayer for rescue from all the ways and works of Satan: from sickness as well as from sin; from pain, the penalty of transgression, as well as from transgression itself.

But, it is asked, if the privilege and promise in this matter are so clear, how is it that the cases of recovery through the prayer of faith; are so rare? Probably because the prayer of faith itself is so rare, and especially because when found it receives almost no support in the Church as a whole. Prayer for such matters should be the outcome of the faith and intercession of the whole body of believers. So it was in the beginning. When Peter was delivered from prison it was because "prayer was made without ceasing of the Church unto God for him." And when Paul knelt alone in the chamber of Publius to intercede for his father's recovery, it was equally true that his petition was an expression of what was the unanimous and concurring faith of the whole Church. But it is not easy for an individual prayer to make headway against the adverse sentiment of the great body of Christians. For example, let an earnest soul pray for a revival in a church where the prevailing view is that of indifferent unbelief, or positive disbelief in revivals, and would he be likely to obtain the coveted blessing? The promise stands fast, indeed, "How much more shall your heavenly Father give the Holy Spirit unto them that ask Him!" but the condition, "They were all with one accord in one place," is wanting. How shall one man move the great ship before the wind by holding up his pocket-handkerchief to the breeze, when all the mariners refuse to spread the sails? And how shall one Christian's faith prevail against the non-consent of the whole Church? There may be scattered instances of blessing in such circumstances, but there can be no widespread exhibitions of Divine power. They tell us that all the heat communicated to a cake of ice short of that which would bring it to the melting point becomes latent and disappears. Faith, likewise, may become inoperative and fruitless in the Church when multiplied a hundredfold by unbelief.

But there is another answer also to the question. It is as true here as in any other field that God acts sovereignly and according to His own determinate counsel. He sees it best to recover one person at the instance of His people's prayers, and He may see it best to withhold such recovery for the time from another.[28] And we would most strongly emphasize the importance of offering our supplications for this, as for all mercies, in the most loyal and hearty and unreserved submission to the will of our Father. He has told us that "all things work together for good to them that love God," but we are not to conclude that they all work in one direction. There are blessings and trials, joys and sorrows, pains and pleasures, sickness and health, falls and recoveries, advances and retrogressions, but the final issue and resultant of all these experiences is our highest good. This we conceive to be the meaning of the promise. And when we remember that God superintends all this complex system of providences, and foresees the final effect of each separate element in it, we see how becoming it is that we should bring every petition into subjection to the will of the Lord. When Augustine was contemplating leaving Africa and going into Italy, his pious mother, fearing the effect which the seductions of Rome might have upon his ardent nature, besought the Lord with many tears and cries that he might not be permitted to go. He was suffered to go, however, and in Milan he found his soul's salvation. "Thou didst deny her," says Augustine in his confessions, "Thou didst deny her what she prayed for at that time that Thou mightest grant her what she prayed for always." This is a perfect illustration of the point which we are emphasizing. God may withhold the recovery which we ask today because He will give to us that "saving health" which we ask always. He may permit temporal death to come, in order that He may preserve His child unto life eternal. How little we can know what is best for us and what shall work our highest good! Isaac Barrow, the eminent and devout theologian, was so wayward and wicked while a lad that his Christian father confessed he had prayed that "if it pleased God to take away any of his children it might be his son Isaac." What would the Church have lost had this prayer been granted? On the other hand, the mother of Charles I., it is said, bent above the cradle of her infant boy when he had been given up to die, and refused to be comforted unless God would spare his life. His life was spared: but how gladly would that mother have had it otherwise could she have looked forward to the day when his head fell bleeding and ghastly beneath the stroke of the executioner's axe! Such illustrations open a broad field for reflection, and

---

[28] "Nor are signs wrought continually, but as often as it shall have pleased God and seems necessary; whence it is evident that to work signs depends not on the option of man, but on the will of God." Bullinger.

suggest the real limitation of the prayer of faith as related to healing—viz., the gracious and all-wise will of God.

And this is the same limitation which belongs to the entire realm of intercessory prayer. "Holding such views in regard to the efficacy of prayer for recovery from disease, why should you have any sick persons in your flock?" is the question which a clerical critic propounds. We shall answer by propounding a much harder one. Holding such views in regard to the efficacy of prayer for the conversion of souls, and resting on the plain declaration of Scripture concerning God our Savior that He "will have all men to be saved and to come to the knowledge of the truth, "why should our questioner allow any sinner to remain unconverted under his ministry? And yet is it not his sorrowful experience that of all that come under his word and prayers only a few comparatively give evidence of being regenerated? Alas that we must all concede that this is our observation! But because I have to admit that all will not hear, and all will not repent and be converted, shall I therefore refuse to persist in preaching and warning and rebuke and intercession, "that I might by all means save some"? Indeed not! And since the sure word of promise is given to us on this matter also, let us hold fast our confidence without wavering, so that whether there be few or many who shall be recovered we may by all means heal some. Such we believe to be a candid verdict in regard to the promise concerning prayer for the sick.

And now, what shall be said in regard to the testimony brought forward? It would be considered very weighty, we venture to believe, were it adduced in support of a generally accepted theory. When evidence and established conviction are put in the same scale, they tip the beam very easily, but testimony against a heavy make-weight of unbelief and prejudice makes slow headway. If the story of Augustine, or Luther, or Livingstone, or Fox, or Dorothea Trudel were found in the Gospels, how we should fight for its genuineness! "Ah! yes," you say, "because the Gospels are inspired, and we should not dare to question any statement recorded on their pages." But miracles were given to accredit inspiration, and not inspiration to accredit miracles. The first miracles got themselves credited simply on human testimony, on the evidence of men and women like ourselves who saw and believed and reported. And when they had become established as facts, then their weight went to prove the Divine origin of Christianity. It is easy for us to say that the works recorded in the Gospels are supernatural because the system to which they belong is supernatural. That is true; but it is reading backward. The first Christians could not reason in that way, because the premise from which we argue was not established in their day. No! The miracles of the New Testament became established in precisely the same manner as any alleged fact is proved today—by the evidence of honest, candid, and truthful witnesses, who saw and bare record. If, therefore, our theologians choose to treat the narratives of such godly and truthful men as Augustine and Luther and Baxter as "silly tales," they must be careful that they do not build a portico to "the school of Hume," in which their pupils will easily and logically graduate from the denial of modern miracles to the denial of all miracles.

Nor does age have anything to do with determining the value of signs and wonders. A young miracle is entitled to the same respect as an old one, provided it bears the same credentials. And if we give way to the subtle illusion that the marvelous is to be credited just in proportion to its distance from us—if we show ourselves forward to admit that the Lord wrought great and mighty signs eighteen hundred years ago, and utterly averse to conceding that the same Lord does anything of the kind today—then we must be very careful again that we do not give countenance to the mythical theory of miracles, which has been so strongly pushed in this generation. Do we believe that the credibility of miracles depends on the magnifying power of distance? that antiquity must stand behind them as a kind of convex mirror to render them sufficiently large to be distinctly seen? How we revolt from such an imputation! Yet let us be cautious that we do not give occasion for it, by emphasizing, as we cannot too strongly, the great things that the Lord did by our fathers, while we utterly refuse to believe that He does any such things by their sons. Let us not forget that the Jews in Christ's day were condemned for denying the wonderful works wrought in their own generation, and not for disbelieving those done by Elijah and Elisha nine hundred years before. The defenders of New Testament miracles are numbered by hundreds, and there is no special danger of a breach in the ramparts of Christianity at that point. The question of God's supernatural working today and tomorrow is the one where havoc is being wrought. Unbelief shading off from rationalism to liberal evangelicism is doing its utmost to give away our most precious heritage. With how many is regeneration merely a repairing of the old nature by culture, instead of a miraculous communication of the Divine life! How many regard the promised coming of Christ in glory as simply a new phase of providence effected by the turning of the kaleidoscope of history! To how many is Satan only a concrete symbol of evil, so that their denial of the reality of the infernal has issued in a disbelief in the Supernal! To how many is inspiration only a higher state of intellectual exaltation; and resurrection an elimination or spiritual release, effected by the dissolving chemistry of death! To read the utterances put forth by Christian teachers in these directions within the last few years is enough to startle one and make him cry out in the strong words of Edward Irving: "O the serpent cunning of this liberal spirit!—it is killing our children; it has already slain its tens of thousands; this city is sick unto death, and dying of the mortal wounds which she hath received from it." Therefore let us be cautious that, by taking up the current sneer about prodigies and wonders, we do not get our eyes blinded and our ears dull of hearing so as to be utterly unable to discern any Divine manifestations in case they should be made.

As to the practice involved in this discussion: Can it be of any service for authenticating the truth of Christianity today to show examples of men and women healed of sickness through faith in the Great Physician? So far as our observation goes, the most powerful effect of such experiences is upon the subjects themselves, in the marked consecration and extraordinary spiritual anointing which almost invariably attend them. We can bear unqualified testimony on this point. Of a large number within the circle of our acquaintance who have been healed, or who have imagined themselves healed, we have never seen one who did not give evidence of having received an unusual endowment of spiritual power. It has seemed as though the double blessing of forgiveness and health had been followed by the bestowment of a double portion of the Spirit. If we could let the objectors to our doctrine witness some of the examples of alleged healing which have been under our eyes for several years—inebriates who, after half a lifetime wasted in desperate struggles for reform, declare that their appetite was instantly eradicated in answer to intercessory prayer; invalids lifted in an hour from couches where they had lain for years; and now their adoring gratitude, their joyful self-surrender, their burning zeal in the service of the Lord—if we could let our critics witness these things, we believe that the most stubborn among them would at least be willing that these happy subjects of— something—should remain under the illusion that they have had the Savior's healing touch laid upon them.

Such we believe to be the verdict of candor upon this whole question. We do not ask that the highest place in Christian doctrine be given to faith in supernatural healing. We readily admit that grace is vastly more important than miracles; but miracles have their place as shadows of greater things. We urge that they may hold this place, that we may be helped thereby the better to apprehend the substance.

When the Emperor Theodosius had on a great occasion given release to all the prisoners confined within his realm, he exclaimed: "And now would to God I could open all the tombs and give life to the dead!" If we could sometimes see the Lord unlocking the prison-house of sickness and giving reprieve from the impending penalty of death to those long in bondage, it might be a salutary pledge and reminder of our Redeemer's purpose to bring forth the prisoners from the tomb in that day when He shall quicken our mortal bodies by his Spirit that dwelleth in us: it might sound in our ears with repeated emphasis the Lord's word, "Turn ye to the stronghold, ye prisoners of hope; even today do I declare that I will render double unto thee."

# Chapter 11
# THE VERDICT OF CAUTION

"The Church can no longer say, 'Silver and gold have I none,'" said Pope Gregory to Thomas Aquinas. "No, nor can she say any longer, 'In the name of Jesus Christ of Nazareth rise up and walk,'" answered Thomas. A very deep wisdom and a very fruitful suggestion are contained in this answer of the theologian. As riches increase, that close dependence on God, which is the fertile soil of faith and trust, decreases. It is when we are most straitened in ourselves that the bounty of God is most widely open to us; it is when we have nothing that we find the key with which to enter in and possess all things which are ours in Christ.

We are living in an age in which the Church enjoys very large prosperity in an earthly direction; when she is "rich and increased in goods," and therefore in constant peril of saying, "I have need of nothing." It is not an era, therefore, in which the greatest triumphs of faith and intercession may be reasonably looked for. Every Christian knows in his own experience the difference between saying his prayers and supplicating God for help under the stress of overwhelming need; and in the Church we may well open our eyes to the fact that our prosperity and our rest from persecution and trial are sources of weakness and enervation. We do not pray as apostles and martyrs and confessors and reformers prayed, because not pressed upon by enemies, and thereby shut up to God as they were; and so we do not get such answers as they received.

Our first caution therefore concerning this subject is that we do not demand too much of the Christian Church of today. We should ask great things and expect great things of God; but of men, weak and backslidden in heart, we ought not to be too exacting. Faith for healing cannot rise above the general level of the Church's faith. There are multitudes of prayers in these days, written prayers and extemporaneous prayers, prayers in the Church and prayers in the family; but how many Christians out of the great mass have any very extensive record of direct, definite, and unmistakable answers to their petitions? Of all who knock at the gates of heaven each day, how many wait and watch till the door is opened and their portion is brought to them? But it is not reasonable to expect that such as have no experience in prevailing prayers for other things should be able to wield at once the prayer of faith which saves the sick. In God's school it is no more true than in man's, that pupils can step immediately into the highest attainments with no previous study or diligent mastery of the first principles of faith. If the conviction and assurance of the Church as a whole should rise to the height of this great argument, we might witness wonderful things; buts so long as it does not, we should not be made to doubt because of the meager conquests which we witness. It is for us to pray always and earnestly that the Lord would be pleased to restore to His Church her primitive gifts by restoring her primitive endowments of unworldliness and poverty of spirit and separation unto God. If any organ of the body be weak and sickly, the only sure method of restoring it is to tone up the whole system, and bring it to the normal standard of health; so if the entire body of Christ were revived and reinvested with her first spiritual powers, these special gifts and functions of which we are writing would not fail to be in extensive exercise.

Then, again, we need to be very careful that we do not fall into heresy on this question. Heresy, as a thoughtful Christian writer has pointed out, means a dividing or a choosing; it is the acceptance and advocacy of one hemisphere of truth to the rejection of the other. Every doctrine is two-sided; so that whichever phase commends itself to us we must remember its counterpart, and aim to preserve the balance of truth by holding fast to this also. In the matter before us, as in the whole doctrine of prayer, human freedom and the Divine sovereignty are inseparably joined. Here are the two sides:

"Ask what ye will and it shall be done unto you." John 15:7.

"If we ask anything according to His will He heareth us." 1 John 5:14.

In our assent to the doctrine of the Divine sovereignty we must never forget the gracious privilege which is accorded to us of freely making known our requests to God, with the fullest assurance that He will hear and grant them. "Whatsoever ye shall ask in my name that will I do;"—we cannot lean too hard upon this promise or plead it too confidently. But at the same time we must be sure that beneath every prayer the strong, clear undertone of "Thy will be done" is distinctly heard. Of course, in saying this we open a mystery and suggest a seeming contradiction which the wisdom of the ages has been unable to solve.

But because we find both sides of this truth distinctly expressed in Scripture, we must be sure to emphasize both.[29] Let us be very careful, therefore, that we do not proclaim the doctrine of Divine healing in an unbalanced and reckless manner. If we are told that a brother in the church is sick, let us not make undue haste to declare that he will certainly be restored if we carry his case to God. We must keep distinctly in mind both Melita and Miletum: remembering that at one place Paul healed the father of Publius by his prayers, and that at the other place he left Trophimus sick. Some commentators have conjectured the reason why the latter was not at that time recovered—viz., that he was to be thereby

---

[29] "The only way for a believer, if he wants to go rightly, is to remember that truth is always two-sided. If there is any truth that the Holy Ghost has specially pressed upon your heart, if you do not want to push it to the extreme, ask what is the counter-truth, and lean a little of your weight upon that; otherwise, if you bear so very much on one side of the truth, there is a danger of pushing it into a heresy. Heresy means selected truth; it does not mean error: heresy and error are very different things. Heresy is truth; but truth pushed into undue importance, to the disparagement of the truth on the other side." William Lincoln.

kept back from martyrdom, which he would probably have met had he gone with Paul, and for which his time had not come in the purpose of God. Whether there is any truth or not in this conjecture, there was doubtless some good reason why this companion of the apostle should have been detained for the while under infirmity. The all-wise and gracious Lord, who is shaping our lives, must be allowed to choose such detentions for us, if He sees that he can thereby best forward our usefulness and advance His own glory. We should be cautious therefore that in this matter we do not push the element of human choice too strongly and rashly, to the ignoring of the Divine, and so bring in the heresy of free-will.

Let us take warning from those misguided teachers who are going to the other extreme, and bearing so hard upon the Divine sovereignty as practically to deny man's freedom to ask or expect miraculous healing. More than this, indeed, they seem to have pushed the sovereignty of God almost into an iron fixedness, where even the Almighty is not at liberty to work miracles any longer, as though under bonds to restrain this office of His Omnipotence since the apostolic age. This we hold to be a far more serious error than the other, since it appears not only to shut up man's freedom of asking, but to limit God's freedom of giving. There have appeared in our religious newspapers, of late, extended deliverances, in which the possibility of any miraculous interventions in this age is most emphatically denied, and the attempt to apply the plain promise in James to present times and circumstances characterized as gross superstition. A rash responsibility for evangelical teachers to take in speaking thus, we should say. It is opening channels of denial respecting the supernatural, into which the swelling unbelief of our age will not be slow to pour, inevitably deepening those channels into great gulfs of scepticism.

"Ah! but it is you who are ministering to unbelief," it is replied, "by holding out promises in the fulfilment of which men will be disappointed, and thereby be led to doubt the word of the Lord." That is an objection that can be urged equally against the whole doctrine of prayer, and it is one concerning which we can take no blame. It is for us simply to emphasize every promise which God has given, and to refrain from encumbering it with any condition of ours. If such assent should promote unbelief in any, that is the Lord's responsibility who gave the promise. If instead of assent we give denial, that is our responsibility, and the consequences must lie at our door.

Let us on our part, therefore, avoid heresy by keeping these two great elements of prayer in equilibrium,—believing strongly but asking submissively, holding up in one hand of our supplication a "Thus saith the Lord," and in the other a "The will of the Lord be done."

It requires great caution also in this subject that we do not fall into fanaticism. As we have already indicated, fanaticism is not necessarily a sign of error. It is more likely to be a healthful than a fatal symptom. It is often the proud flesh and fever heat which indicate that healing is going on in some fractured bone or ligament of the system of doctrine. Nevertheless it must be subdued and kept down, lest the truth may suffer reproach. And in this field especially do we need to guard against it.

Nowhere does zeal require to be so carefully tempered by knowledge as here. Novices, lifted up with pride, will lay hold of this doctrine, and with the enthusiasm which the discovery of some long-neglected truth is apt to engender, they will parade their faith, and make extravagant claims concerning it. Nothing needs to be held with such quietness and reserve as this truth. To press it upon the undevout and uninstructed is only to bring it into contempt. Those who have the most wisdom in such matters will be found speaking in very hushed tones, and without assumption or ostentation. One who has the habit of parading this theme on all occasions, and haranguing it at every street corner, gives clear evidence of his unfitness to handle it. Here is a serious peril, as we foresee; but the best truth has always had to run such risks. Dry and lifeless tradition is the only thing which has invariably been exempt from them.

The more careful, therefore, should all be, who desire to see God's word prevail, to pray much and argue little, that the Spirit who can alone discover the deep things of God may reveal His true will to the Church concerning this important question. And most especially is all undue forwardness in attempting to exercise this ministry to be avoided. We are persuaded that there is no deeper or more difficult question which can come within our reach. If any one is sincerely desirous of being used of the Lord in this direction, let him give diligent heed to be taught of God concerning it. We are persuaded that there is no school on earth which is competent to graduate one in this Divine science. Therefore we would commend our readers neither to books nor to theologians, but to the personal instructions of the Spirit of God. We admire the candor with which one eminent doctor of theology, Professor Godet, has confessed the true secret of knowledge in this field. He says: "A single prayer answered, a single case of living contact with the power of the Father, a single exertion of the strength of Christ over the weakness that is in us, will teach us more on the subject of miracles than all that I have been able in this lecture to say to you upon this great subject."

Let it be distinctly borne in mind that this is no easy art, no surface-truth to be picked up by any religious adventurer who may desire to exhibit some novel accomplishment. Unless one is ready for the most absolute self-surrender and the most implicit obedience, let him not even enter this school of inquiry with any hope of learning its secrets. It is told of Pastor Blumhardt, who knew as much of this subject, we believe, as any man in recent times, that after the promise for healing was first brought powerfully to his mind he passed two years in repeated prayers and fastings and searchings for the mind of the Spirit before he had the assurance that he should lay hands on the sick for their recovery. We know that others who have been greatly owned of God in this direction have had a similar experience. Therefore we would interpose a strong caution against rashness or forwardness in this matter. We need less praying for the sick rather than more;

only that the less shall be real, and deep, and intelligent, and believing. What a revelation is contained in the fact that some of the disputants in this controversy, after boldly denying that miraculous healing is possible in this age of the world, have then added, "Of course we ought to pray for the sick!" That is, being fairly interpreted, after becoming thoroughly convinced that God will not interpose supernaturally for their restoration, then we should offer our supplication for their healing. It seems to us, on the contrary, that such a conviction furnishes a good reason why we should refrain from praying till we have acknowledged our unbelief and forsaken it.

The strongest and most enlightened faith, oneness of heart in all uniting to pray, minute and obedient submission to every condition named in Scripture, are what are absolutely essential in this field. With the utmost tenderness and deference we would allude to a memorable instance of praying for the sick, which is fresh in mind. A call issued by the secular authorities; a day of prayer in which believers and formalists alike unite; the incense of the Catholic mass ascending with the intercessions of the Protestant prayer-meeting; the Jew and the Christian offering up, each according to his kind; the helpless and imprisoned patient meantime shut out from the ministry of grace and shut in to the ministry of drugs and stimulants, so that any lucid exercise of faith or of prayer in the Holy Spirit would seem to be well-nigh impossible,—what shall we say of this? God forbid that we should by the slightest criticism seem to mock the grief of a suffering nation, or to disparage a call to prayer from the rulers who did the best they knew in a great crisis! And we have no light as to how the Lord may have regarded such an offering. But in simple candor and loyalty to the word of God we must decline to have this event established as a prayer-gauge, as many are insisting on making it. It was simply a national fast day, concerning which we proffer no remark. But the prayer of faith, by the elders of the church, offered at the special request of the sick person, made in the name of Jesus, the one Mediator between God and man, and in the Holy Ghost the Comforter, and all rendered up in obedience to every known condition of faith and oneness of mind enjoined in Scripture—this is the kind of prayer for the sick which we are discussing in this volume, and no other. Here is a service which belongs to the Holy of holies of the Christian Church, and which cannot be brought out into the court of the Gentiles.

A caution against dogmatism and pride of opinion in a field where we know only in part may well close what we have to say. Alas! how little we truly understand of this whole matter! We believe strongly because we have promises that are "yea, and in Him amen, unto the glory of God by us."

And so we have presented as best we could the doctrine, the history, and the experience of the Church upon this great question. How little we can speak of actual use of these gifts! But in the oft-quoted words of a good man, we are "very confident that the Lord has more truth yet to break forth out of His holy word,"—on this subject especially, because so many of God's people are "searching diligently what or what manner of time the Spirit of Christ did signify," when He penned these great promises. If God has anything to reveal by any instrument whatever, let us be open to receive it. If such instruments shall prove to be, as we quite believe, the "poor of this world rich in faith;" the servants of Christ, who after long endurance of the bondage of pain have traced the promises of healing line by line in their own experience; and the obedient children, who have faced the world's doubt and scornful denial for the joy of answering God's challenge, "Prove me now herewith,"—let us take heed that we do not despise even such teachers and light-bearers. And in all our urgency for the truth of God in this matter, let us not forget that miracles are but signs, not the substance. In prayer, in preaching, in tears and persuasions over perishing souls, in bearing the cross and counting all things as loss for the excellency of the knowledge of Christ Jesus the Lord, let us for the present be diligently employed, until the day dawn and the shadows flee away; until the harvest be gathered and the firstfruits shall be needed no more; until that which is perfect shall come, and that which is in part shall be done away.

# Chapter 12

# THE CONCLUSION

The prayer of faith, when really understood and exercised, will be confessed to be the very highest attainment of the Christian life. And yet it is an attainment which comes from unlearning rather than from learning; from self-abnegation rather than from self-culture; from decrease towards spiritual childhood rather than from increase towards the stature of intellectual manhood. The same condition holds for opening the kingdom of heaven for others as for entering it ourselves—viz., that we "become as little children." To reach down and grasp the secret of simplicity of faith and implicitness of confidence is far more difficult than to reach up and lay hold of the key of knowledge. Hence, how significant it is that in the Scriptures children are made the heroes of faith! "This is the victory that overcomes the world, even our faith." And who, then, are the overcomers? Who are they that have laid hold of the mighty secret of this spiritual conquest? "You are of God little children, and have overcome them," And why? "Because greater is He that is in you than He that is in them." Yes; and just in proportion as we are emptied of self, and schooled back into that second childhood which should follow the second birth, will God be in us most fully and act through us most powerfully.

There is a passage in the life of an eminent Christian philosopher which is well worth pondering deeply and seriously in this age of superficial praying. A friend of Coleridge says that, standing by his bedside not long before his death, he was commenting on the Lord's Prayer, when he suddenly broke out: "Oh, my dear friend, to pray, to pray as God would have us; to pray with all the heart and strength, with the reason and the will, to believe vividly that God will listen to your voice through Christ, and verily do the thing He pleases thereupon—this is the last, the greatest achievement of the Christian's warfare on earth! Teach us to pray, O Lord!" "And then," says the narrator, "he burst into a flood of tears, and begged me to pray for him." The greatest achievement indeed! And yet it is not by might nor by power. Wisdom cannot compass it; learning cannot master it. "To pray with all the heart and strength,"—which should mean with the heart submerged in the heart of Christ, and with the strength transformed into "the irresistible might of weakness," with the reason brought into complete captivity to the cross of Christ, and with the will surrendered up to the will of God,—this is indeed the secret of power.

Let it be noted that we are speaking of one of the highest attainments of Christianity now, and not of its rudiments. The faith which saves us is the simplest exercise of the heart; the prayer of faith which saves the sick is the most exacting. The one is merely receptive, the other is powerfully self-surrendering.

Do you wish to be saved, the Master will only say to you, "Take the cup of salvation and call upon the name of the Lord." Do you wish to be mightily used of the Lord in the office of raising the sick from their beds, and giving life to those who are dead in sin, you will hear him asking the searching question, "Can you drink of the cup that I drink of and be baptized with the baptism which I am baptized with?" In the faith by which we are converted and delivered from the wrath to come we do nought but receive Jesus Christ; in the faith by which we are consecrated and made vessels "meet for the Master's use and prepared unto every good work," we give ourselves, soul, body, and spirit, to Jesus Christ.

That we may see how strenuous and searching the requirements for prevailing prayer are, let us note three explicit conditions laid down in Scripture, to which are attached the promise of whatsoever we ask:

"If you abide in Me and My words abide in you." John 15:7.

"If we keep His commandments and do those things that are pleasing in His sight." 1 John 3:22.

"If we ask anything according to His will." 1 John 5:14.

The first requirement " If ye abide in Me . . ." is that of intimate and unbroken communion with the Lord. Our justification depends upon our being in Christ. Our power and fellowship depend upon our abiding in Christ. And this last implies the most constant and uninterrupted intimacy of the soul with the Savior. It is the entering into His life, and having His life so entering into us, that the confession of the apostle becomes realized in us—"I live, yet not I, but Christ lives in me." Such abiding will stand in exact proportion to our detachment from the world. The double-minded man, "who is trying to make the most of both worlds, grasping for earth's riches and pleasures and yet wishing to secure the highest prizes of the kingdom of heaven, will inevitably waver; and to such a one the Scripture speaks expressly, "Let not that man think that he shall receive anything of the Lord." It is a hard saying, but one which in some form or other is constantly repeated in the word of God. "Do you not know that the friendship of this world is enmity to God?" asks the apostle James; and the converse is hardly less true for believers, that the enmity of this world is friendship with God. When, for any cause, a Christian finds his earthly affections sundered, so that they do not draw him down, he will at least learn how much easier it is to set his affections on things above. Never do we find the heart of God opening so widely to us as when the heart of the world is closed against us. There is a homely wisdom, therefore, in the lines of an old poet, Henry Vaughan, when for his "soul's chief health" he prays for these three things:

> "A living faith, a heart of flesh,
> The world an enemy;
> The last will keep the first two fresh
> And bring me where I'd be."

How easy it is to understand the secret of Paul's "I live, yet not I," after he has told us of the double crucifixion which he has endured—"By whom the world is crucified unto me and I unto the world." Some become dead to the world through the pain or trial or privation which cuts them off from all communion with it, though the world is still there; to others the world becomes dead because of the cutting off of friends, and comforts, and fortune, in which their world consisted. In either case, if there is a heart which truly longs for God, it will find a wonderful release towards Him. We are advocating no morbid asceticism, but simply interpreting Scripture; and we must add, also, interpreting the secret of power in those who have been mightily prevalent in intercession. For in tracing the lives of those most eminently successful in the prayer of faith, as they have passed in review in this volume, we have found that, almost without exception, they have been those remarkably separated from the world, either through their own voluntary consecration or through persecutions and trials and sufferings endured for Christ's sake.

The next condition which we have noted, "If we keep His commandments and do those things which are pleasing in His sight," needs to be emphasized not less strongly. Implicit obedience, a painstaking attention to the smallest and the greatest requirements of the Lord, is what is enjoined. Rather, we might say, a fidelity in service which admits no distinction of small or great when handling the commandments of the Lord. For true obedience knows no such discriminations as essential and non-essential in the Divine requirements; it has no test fine enough for distinguishing things indifferent from things vital. Among the sayings of Christ, our perfect Exemplar in praying as in living, we find these two professions which we do well to read together:

"I do always those things that please Him."

"I know that You hear Me always."

Here again we touch the heart of this great secret. To obey well is to pray well; for not only does God love the willing and the obedient, but such know His mind and understand how and what to ask as no others can. One step in compliance with the Father's will will carry us farther in knowledge than ten steps in mere studious search into the mystery of His ways. Wonderfully do the mind and purposes of God open themselves to the obedient soul. "Who by searching can find out God?" But "if any man do His will he shall know of the doctrine."

Therefore should we study to exercise the most minute and diligent obedience to the Lord's requirements. "Whatsoever He says to you, do it." In keeping this commandment there is a great reward and the surest entrance into the promise of Christ, "Whatsoever you shall ask the Father in my name He will give it you." In all our Christian life and practice let us beware of saying concerning any command of God that it is only a form, and therefore it does not matter. Forms are sometimes given, no doubt, as tests of our fidelity,—as when Naaman is enjoined to wash seven times in the Jordan for his healing, or when the elders are commanded to anoint the sick with oil for their recovery. Forms are nothing, to be sure; but the obedience which responds to those forms in every minute particular, for the love of Christ, is most precious in the sight of God. Hence, significantly, Paul thanks God concerning the Roman Christians that they had "obeyed from the heart that form of doctrine which was committed to them."

And, finally, "If we ask anything according to His will;" which means "that we should be of a truth purely, simply, and wholly at one with the One Eternal Will of God, or altogether without will, so that the created will should flow out into the Eternal Will, and be swallowed up and lost therein, so that the Eternal Will alone should do and leave undone in us." "Theologia Germanica," p. 90. And let us not be alarmed at this requirement, as though it meant pains, racks, tortures, the loss of our lives, the death of our children, and everything else which is dreadful to contemplate. Why is it that we have associated such things with the prayer, "Thy will be done"? Let us search the Scriptures and see what God's revealed will is. "For this is the will of God, even your sanctification." 1 Thes. 4:3. "And this is the will of Him that sent me, that everyone that sees the Son and believes on Him may have everlasting life." John 6:40. "Who will have all men to be saved and to come unto the knowledge of the truth." 1 Tim. 2:4. These and many other texts, if we had space to quote them, point in one direction, and indicate that the will of God is our health and not our hurt; our weal and not our woe; our life and not our death. It must be the will of God that all that is contrary to Him should be destroyed. "Every plant which my heavenly Father has not planted shall be rooted up." Sin, sickness, and death are contrary to God; they are not plants of His planting, but tares which the enemy has sown in His field. Therefore, they are to be plucked up, and we may be certain that we are working in the line of His will when we are seeking to eradicate them. What, then, if we should chiefly aim in our ministry at the sick bed to set forth this blessed disposition and purpose of the Divine will? What if, instead of laying such stress on patient submission to pain and bodily disorder, as things inevitable, we should seek to lift the sufferer up into harmony with God, in whom there is no sickness and no disorder? And then when we pray "Thy will be done" we shall mean, Let sickness be destroyed; let the sufferer be delivered from the racks and tortures of pain's inquisition; let sin and the bitter fruit of sin in these poor tormented bodies be plucked up together. In praying thus we must surely be setting our faces in the right direction. For looking upward for the key of our petition, "Thy will be done on earth," we hear "as it is in heaven." But in heaven there is certainly no sin, sickness, or death; and so we are enjoined to ask and strive and labor that there be none on earth. And looking forward to the predicted consummation of Christ's redemptive work, when God's will shall be actually done on earth, we read the glowing words, "And there shall be no more death, neither sorrow nor crying, neither shall there be any more pain." Here then is the clearly defined pattern, above us and before us; and amid all the tangled mysteries of evil we should set our faces like a flint to pray it out and work it out into blessed fulfilment. And while we recognize the doctrine of the Divine Sovereignty, to which we have elsewhere referred, this should no more prevent our asking in faith for the healing of our bodies than the doctrine of election should prevent our asking with the fullest assurance for the salvation of our souls. These observations in this closing chapter, let it be remembered, are especially for such as maybe called to exercise the ministry of healing. If there are those who desire this office we believe they should seek with all their heart the consecration, the separation from the world, and the surrender to God's will, which the Scriptures enjoin as conditions of prevailing prayer.

To the sick, sensible of their lack of these attainments, and fearing that their case cannot be reached on that account, we would speak a different word, even the word of the Master—"Be not afraid, only believe." Christ comes to the sinner, helpless, guilty, lost, and saves him just as He finds him. And so with the sufferer, when he lies "stripped of his raiment, wounded, and half dead." As the good Samaritan "came where he was and bound up his wounds, pouring in oil and wine," so Jesus will take the patient just where he is, if He takes him at all. We have not to make ourselves better in order to be healed, either spiritually or physically. Therefore let the sufferer take courage and lift up his weary head. Oh, you unnumbered subjects of pain and bodily torture, with hands and feet which you would use so diligently and swiftly in the service of your Lord if they were only released from the fetters which bind them!—oh, you countless victims of pain and disorder, who have never consecrated either your souls or your bodies to the service of Him who made them,—hear all of you that voice of Him who speaks from heaven saying, "I am the Lord that heals you." And if the promises of God and the teachings of Scripture and the testimonies of the healed set forth in this book might throw one ray of hope or alleviation into your sick chambers, it would repay amply the pains we have taken in its preparation, and more than compensate us for any reproach we may incur for having borne witness to a doctrine of which many, as yet, can hear only with impatience and derision. And to this last word we would join a prayer which has come down to us from a very ancient liturgy:

"REMEMBER, O LORD, THOSE WHO ARE DISEASED AND SICK, AND THOSE WHO ARE TROUBLED BY UNCLEAN SPIRITS; AND DO YOU, WHO ARE GOD, SPEEDILY HEAL AND DELIVER THEM."

# About CrossReach Publications

CROSSREACH
PUBLICATIONS

Thank you for choosing CrossReach Publications.

*Hope. Inspiration. Trust.*

These three words sum up the philosophy of why CrossReach Publications exist. To create inspiration for the present thus inspiring hope for the future, through trusted authors from previous generations.

We are *non-denominational* and *non-sectarian*. We appreciate and respect what every part of the body brings to the table and believe everyone has the right to study and come to their own conclusions. We aim to help facilitate that end.

*We aspire to excellence.* If we have not met your standards please contact us and let us know. We want you to feel satisfied with your product. Something for everyone. We publish quality books both in presentation and content from a wide variety of authors who span various doctrinal positions and traditions, on a wide variety of Christian topics that will teach, encourage, challenge, inspire and equip.

*We're a family-based home-business.* A husband and wife team raising 8 kids. If you have any questions or comments about our publications email us at:

ContactUs@CrossReach.net

Don't forget you can follow us on Facebook and Twitter, (links are on the copyright page above) to keep up to date on our newest titles and deals.

# Bestselling Titles from CrossReach[30]

A. W. TOZER

HOW TO BE

*Filled*
WITH
THE
*Holy Spirit*

CrossReach Publications

## How to Be Filled with the Holy Spirit
A. W. Tozer

Before we deal with the question of how to be filled with the Holy Spirit, there are some matters which first have to be settled. As believers you have to get them out of the way, and right here is where the difficulty arises. I have been afraid that my listeners might have gotten the idea somewhere that I had a how-to-be-filled-with-the-Spirit-in-five-easy-lessons doctrine, which I could give you. If you can have any such vague ideas as that, I can only stand before you and say, "I am sorry"; because it isn't true; I can't give you such a course. There are some things, I say, that you have to get out of the way, settled.

## God Still Speaks
A. W. Tozer

GOD STILL
SPEAKS

A. W. TOZER

Tozer is as popular today as when he was living on the earth. He is respected right across the spectrum of Christianity, in circles that would disagree sharply with him doctrinally. Why is this? A. W. Tozer was a man who knew the voice of God. He shared this experience with every true child of God. With all those who are called by the grace of God to share in the mystical union that is possible with Him through His Son Jesus.

Tozer fought against much dryness and formality in his day. Considered a mighty man of God by most Evangelicals today, he was unconventional in his approach to spirituality and had no qualms about consulting everyone from Catholic Saints to German Protestant mystics for inspiration on how to experience God more fully.

Tozer, just like his Master, doesn't fit neatly into our theological boxes. He was a man after God's own heart and was willing to break the rules (man-made ones that is) to get there.

Here are two writings by Tozer that touch on the heart of this goal. Revelation is Not Enough and The Speaking Voice. A bonus chapter The Menace of the Religious Movie is included.

---

This is meat to sink your spiritual teeth into. Tozer's writings will show you the way to satisfy your spiritual hunger.

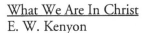

## What We Are In Christ
E. W. Kenyon

I was surprised to find that the expressions "in Christ," "in whom," and "in Him" occur more than 130 times in the New Testament. This is the heart of the Revelation of Redemption given to Paul.

Here is the secret of faith—faith that conquers, faith that moves mountains. Here is the secret of the Spirit's guiding us into all reality. The heart craves intimacy with the Lord Jesus and with the Father. This craving can now be satisfied.

Ephesians 1:7:"In whom we have our redemption through his blood, the remission of our trespasses according to the riches of his grace."

It is not a beggarly Redemption, but a real liberty in Christ that we have now. It is a Redemption by the God Who could say, "Let there be lights in the firmament of heaven," and cause the whole starry heavens to leap into being in a single instant. It is Omnipotence beyond human reason. This is where philosophy has never left a footprint.

## Claiming Our Rights
E. W. Kenyon

There is no excuse for the spiritual weakness and poverty of the Family of God when the wealth of Grace and Love of our great Father with His power and wisdom are all at our disposal. We are not coming to the Father as a tramp coming to the door begging for food; we come as sons not only claiming our legal rights but claiming the natural rights of a child that is begotten in love. No one can hinder us or question our right of approach to our Father.

Satan has Legal Rights over the sinner that God cannot dispute or challenge. He can sell them as slaves; he owns them, body, soul and spirit. But the moment we are born again... receive Eternal Life, the nature of God,—his legal dominion ends.

Christ is the Legal Head of the New Creation, or Family of God, and all the Authority that was given Him, He has given us: (Matthew 28:18), "All authority in heaven," the seat of authority, and "on earth," the place of execution of authority. He is "head over all things," the highest authority in the Universe, for the benefit of the Church which is His body.

THE TWO
BABYLONS

COMPLETE AND
UNABRIDGED

ALEXANDER HISLOP

The Two Babylons
Alexander Hislop

Fully Illustrated High Res. Images. Complete and Unabridged.
Expanded Seventh Edition. This is the first and only seventh edition available in a modern digital edition. Nothing is left out! New material not found in the first six editions!!! Available in eBook and paperback edition exclusively from CrossReach Publications.

"In his work on "The Two Babylons" Dr. Hislop has proven conclusively that all the idolatrous systems of the nations had their origin in what was founded by that mighty Rebel, the beginning of whose kingdom was Babel (Gen. 10:10)."—A. W. Pink, The Antichrist (1923)

There is this great difference between the works of men and the works of God, that the same minute and searching investigation, which displays the defects and imperfections of the one, brings out also the beauties of the other. If the most finely polished needle on which the art of man has been expended be subjected to a microscope, many inequalities, much roughness and clumsiness, will be seen. But if the microscope be brought to bear on the flowers of the field, no such result appears. Instead of their beauty diminishing, new beauties and still more delicate, that have escaped the naked eye, are forthwith discovered; beauties that make us appreciate, in a way which otherwise we could have had little conception of, the full force of the Lord's saying, "Consider the lilies of the field, how they grow; they toil not, neither do they spin: and yet I say unto you, That even Solomon, in all his glory, was not arrayed like one of these." The same law appears also in comparing the Word of God and the most finished productions of men. There are spots and blemishes in the most admired productions of human genius. But the more the Scriptures are searched, the more minutely they are studied, the more their perfection appears; new beauties are brought into light every day; and the discoveries of science, the researches of the learned, and the labours of infidels, all alike conspire to illustrate the wonderful harmony of all the parts, and the Divine beauty that clothes the whole. If this be the case with Scripture in general, it is especially the case with prophetic Scripture. As every spoke in the wheel of Providence revolves, the prophetic symbols start into still more bold and beautiful relief. This is very strikingly the case with the prophetic language that forms the groundwork and corner-stone of the present work. There never has been any difficulty in the mind of any enlightened Protestant in identifying the woman "sitting on seven mountains," and having on her forehead the name written, "Mystery, Babylon the Great," with the Roman apostacy.

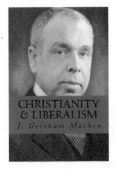

## Christianity and Liberalism
J. Gresham Machen

The purpose of this book is not to decide the religious issue of the present day, but merely to present the issue as sharply and clearly as possible, in order that the reader may be aided in deciding it for himself. Presenting an issue sharply is indeed by no means a popular business at the present time; there are many who prefer to fight their intellectual battles in what Dr. Francis L. Patton has aptly called a "condition of low visibility." Clear-cut definition of terms in religious matters, bold facing of the logical implications of religious views, is by many persons regarded as an impious proceeding. May it not discourage contribution to mission boards? May it not hinder the progress of consolidation, and produce a poor showing in columns of Church statistics? But with such persons we cannot possibly bring ourselves to agree. Light may seem at times to be an impertinent intruder, but it is always beneficial in the end. The type of religion which rejoices in the pious sound of traditional phrases, regardless of their meanings, or shrinks from "controversial" matters, will never stand amid the shocks of life. In the sphere of religion, as in other spheres, the things about which men are agreed are apt to be the things that are least worth holding; the really important things are the things about which men will fight.

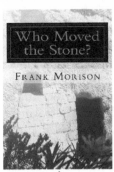

## Who Moved the Stone?
Frank Morison

This study is in some ways so unusual and provocative that the writer thinks it desirable to state here very briefly how the book came to take its present form.

In one sense it could have taken no other, for it is essentially a confession, the inner story of a man who originally set out to write one kind of book and found himself compelled by the sheer force of circumstances to write another.

It is not that the facts themselves altered, for they are recorded imperishably in the monuments and in the pages of human history. But the interpretation to be put upon the facts underwent a change. Somehow the perspective shifted—not suddenly, as in a flash of insight or inspiration, but slowly, almost imperceptibly, by the very stubbornness of the facts themselves.

The book as it was originally planned was left high and dry, like those Thames barges when the great river goes out to meet the incoming sea. The writer discovered one day that not only could he no longer write the book as he had once conceived it, but that he would not if he could.

To tell the story of that change, and to give the reasons for it, is the main purpose of the following pages.

## Elementary Geography
Charlotte Mason

This little book is confined to very simple "reading lessons upon the Form and Motions of the Earth, the Points of the Compass, the Meaning of a Map: Definitions."

It is hoped that these reading lessons may afford intelligent teaching, even in the hands of a young teacher.

Children should go through the book twice, and should, after the second reading, be able to answer any of the questions from memory.

## The Person and Work of the Holy Spirit
R. A. Torey

Before one can correctly understand the work of the Holy Spirit, he must first of all know the Spirit Himself. A frequent source of error and fanaticism about the work of the Holy Spirit is the attempt to study and understand His work without first of all coming to know Him as a Person.

It is of the highest importance from the standpoint of worship that we decide whether the Holy Spirit is a Divine Person, worthy to receive our adoration, our faith, our love, and our entire surrender to Himself, or whether it is simply an influence emanating from God or a power or an illumination that God imparts to us. If the Holy Spirit is a person, and a Divine Person, and we do not know Him as such, then we are robbing a Divine Being of the worship and the faith and the love and the surrender to Himself which are His due.

## In His Steps
Charles M. Sheldon

The sermon story, In His Steps, or "What Would Jesus Do?" was first written in the winter of 1896, and read by the author, a chapter at a time, to his Sunday evening congregation in the Central Congregational Church, Topeka, Kansas. It was then printed as a serial in The Advance (Chicago), and its reception by the readers of that paper was such that the publishers of The Advance made arrangements for its appearance in book form. It was their desire, in which the author heartily joined, that the story might reach as many readers as possible, hence succeeding editions of paper-covered volumes at a price within the reach of nearly all readers.

The story has been warmly and thoughtfully welcomed by Endeavor societies, temperance organizations, and Y. M. C. A. 's. It is the earnest prayer of the author that the book may go its way with a great blessing to the churches for the quickening of Christian discipleship, and the hastening of the Master's kingdom on earth.

Charles M. Sheldon.
Topeka, Kansas,
November, 1897.

WE OFFER A LARGE & GROWING SELECTION OF CHRISTIAN TITLES
ALL AVAILABLE THROUGH AMAZON & OTHER ONLINE STORES
JUST SEARCH FOR CROSSREACH PUBLICATIONS!

Made in United States
Troutdale, OR
08/06/2023

11865459R00065